DEVELOPING PSYCHIC ABILITIES

by

APRYL J. DOUGLAS

Published by TEC Publications
P.O. Box 189601
Sacramento, CA 95818

First Printing 1987
Printed in the United States of America

Cover by Constance McLennan

Self-published in 1985

ISBN: 0-937533-07-6
Library of Congress Catalogue No.: 87-050497

CONTENTS

AUTHOR'S NOTE

It is my hope that the knowledge contained in this book will be of benefit to all who read it. I have tried to be as inclusive and concise as possible.

For those wishing to explore the subject more fully I have included a list of Suggested Reading Material.

It has been my observation after reading a number of books on Metaphysics and Psychic Development, that there is nothing better than the practical application of development techniques to obtain a genuine learning experience from which to grow.

This book is an attempt to give you that learning experience by guiding you through the "how-tos" and "whys" of Metaphysical Awareness. Development techniques are included in nearly every chapter.

Since each chapter strongly supplements the information related in subsequent chapters, it is highly recommended that you read the chapters in sequence to receive the most benefit. In this manner your psychic abilities will unfold in a natural progression. As you go along please refer to the glossary at the end of the book for any unfamiliar words. This way you will become familiar with them and it will help in understanding the chapters.

A section has been prepared for recording any psychic or metaphysical experiences that you may encounter as well as a journal for Psychic Development Exercises.

It is my hope that this book will guide each person who reads it, up the ladder to metaphysical enlightenment by helping to unfold their psychic abilities. [*3]

ABOUT THE AUTHOR

Her intuitive abilities surfaced at the age of thirteen. She has been involved in the study and practice of metaphysics and psychic phenomena since 1967. As Director of Vision Quest Metaphysical Book Store in Canoga Park, CA, she currently conducts lectures on parapsychology, psychic development classes and sponsors a monthly psychic/holistic festival. Also a holistic healing practitioner, and psychic counselor, she utilizes guided imagery meditation/hypnosis and creative visualization as techniques for stress reduction, energy balancing and past life regressions.

Apryl J. Douglas
Vision Quest Metaphysical Book Store
7210 Vassar Ave.
Canoga Park, CA 91303
(818) 888-0487

Please call or write, regarding the following:
Classes, Lectures, Pvt. Readings, Monthly Activities.
To order books, or Refills for Journal Worksheets,
To be put on the Mailing List,
To offer Suggestions, and/or Corrections, for this Book.

DEDICATION

TO MY STUDENTS: Past — Present — Future

*** ACKNOWLEDGEMENTS ***

I want to especially thank my mother and father, Valeree and Scott Douglas, Sr., who have always been supportive of my metaphysical development.

I also wish to acknowledge those persons who have been instrumental in my growth and development in the metaphysical and psychic fields.

> Scott Douglas, Jr. ...... My Godfather in "Santeria."
> Selma Martinez .... My Godmother in "Santeria."
> The Edwards Metaphysical Center:
> Lucille Edwards/Sally Pearson .... My instructors.
> Budd & Patsy Scholtens ....My personal friends who informed me about Psychic Surgery
> Don Casey .... Tour Conductor for the Philippines trip, who arranged for me to photograph the "surgeries" in the "Healing Room."

I want to thank all of the people who have contributed to the growth and development of Vision Quest Metaphysical Center, by sharing their time, energy, and ideas — especially during the preparation of this text.

PREFACE

In 1966, at the age of 13, I began to discover my psychic potential. The first experience being in precognitive dream form.

There I was, standing in the middle of an old Venice Beach, California, one-room flat. I recalled watching Cybil, a friend of the renter, walking across the room in my direction. As she passed, I noticed that she was wearing a black patch over her left eye. Just then as I looked to another area, I was shocked to see Sonny lying on the floor, face down. He had been shot.

Awakened from the shock of it all, I found myself crying hysterically. Instinctively I knew that I must go there to see if everything was all right. Previously I had been given the key for access to the apartment. Somehow, when standing at the door, I couldn't bring myself to walk right in. I knocked, apprehensive of what I might find. As the door slowly opened I peeked inside and cautiously entered. My heart pounded as the rerun of my dream began.

There was Cybil, going through the motions to the tee. "Where's Sonny?" I asked. "Oh, he left. Barbara tried to shoot him," she answered. Thank God that segment didn't come true. I was so relieved to know that he hadn't died that tears streamed from my eyes as I returned home.

Soon after this episode I began to have other clairvoyant experiences. Premonitions would come to me in my thoughts. The first indication that they were beginning appeared to be a distinct physical change in my breathing. If I tried to dismiss the sensation, it became so uncomfortably annoying that it reminded me that what I was experiencing was real. It was only after meditating on what might possibly be happening that I should know more about that the feeling would leave. I was determined to learn more about E.S.P. and psychic phenomena in order to comprehend what was happening to me. I frequently conversed about my new-found interest. I discovered that the experience I had had was not so unusual at all. In fact, it was quite a common occurrence for many. Knowing this somehow seemed to relieve much of my anxiety and fear. My interest seemed to dwindle periodically, only to be renewed as new phenomena occurred.

Soon I was reading every book on the occult and psychic phenomena that I could get my hands on. Years later I attended my first seance. Soon after the seance, in 1975, I even went so far as to be initiated into a spiritualist religion of the Latin culture known as "Santeria." I did this hoping to become enlightened about ceremonial white magic and spiritualism.

It was then that my true psychic abilities began to unfold. One year later, I received "cowrie shells" for divination from my "godparents" in the religion. They showed me how to use them to counsel individuals desiring guidance in their lives. By 1979, a new avenue of learning was unfolding to me. It was the Western cultural approach to modern day metaphysics. I began attending a series of classes at various learning centers. I studied topics such as chakras, auras, the etheric body, prana, color healing, meditation, holistic health, and much more. It has finally become apparent to me that all of the studying I had been doing in metaphysics was for a much higher purpose than just personal enjoyment. It didn't take much to realize that my life was becoming more and more involved with intuitive counseling and healing.

The more knowledge I obtained, the more I wanted to share. In January of 1981, I knew what my road in life was going to be. Determined to share my knowledge and psychic abilities with others, I decided to leave a full-time 10 year established career in banking. This would be the only way to have enough time available to continue studying and working with others in parapsychology and metaphysics.

Over the next three years my energies were strongly devoted to three areas: (1) The teaching of Psychic Development, (2) Metaphysical Healing, (3) Psychic Counseling. I had finally become established in the field and was relatively satisfied with the profession I had chosen.

In January of 1984, I visited my doctor for a routine female examination. During the exam he found some small tumors or cysts in my left breast. This concerned me because at age 18 I had been hospitalized for the removal of one large benign tumor in the same breast and approximate location. My doctor instructed me to have a Xeromammography taken to determine the size of the growths. I did so. However, they were located so close to the breast bone that they did not show up in the X-ray. After speaking with my doctor about the results he told me not to worry. He said that we would monitor the growths periodically in order to keep them in check. He also instructed me to immediately stop eating and drinking any product containing caffeine as it would tend to promote cystic growths.

I then told him that I had an opportunity to go to the Philippines to experience Psychic Surgery by the healers there. He emphatically insisted that I should not go as it was all a big fraud, a gimmick or sleight of hand. I let it go at that for the time being.

During the latter part of January, I received a phone call from a dear friend who knew of my circumstance. Only one year prior, he and his wife had both gone to Manila to be healed by the psychic surgeons there. He informed me that there was a group leaving for the Philippines in about two weeks and gave me the phone number of someone to call should I decide to go.

After very careful deliberation, having weighed all factors including my doctor's opinion, I decided to go to the Philippines. I felt that it was an opportunity offered to me that would enhance my personal growth as well as to give me insight into other areas of my chosen field.

Psychic Surgery is the ability of those chosen as gifted healers, to operate on the human body using only their bare hands as surgical instruments. In this manner, they penetrate deeply below the surface of the skin and physically remove diseased or damaged tissue, blood clots, cysts, tumors, and scar tissue. They do not, however, perform reconstructive or cosmetic surgery. They feel that their gift should be used only to heal the body. It is the old saying, "Beauty is only skin deep."

The group stayed in a Manila hotel for two weeks. Every day, except on Sunday, there were two healing sessions. All healings were performed on the hotel premises. The sponsor for the healers was an organized travel service whose only function was to bring those in need of healing to the hotel from wherever they resided in the world. Psychic Surgery is legal in the Philippines. However, at this time it is not legal in the United States.

Next comes the question of fees. I must say that I was impressed with their method of payment for services rendered. Believe it or not, all fees were given completely by anonymous donation based on the individuals' ability to pay. There was never a set fee or suggested donation. It was a matter of giving from the heart for the help you received.

During that two week period I was permitted to remain in the Healing Room and I photographed at least three hundred body-enterings (surgeries) that were performed on the other members of my group. At times, I was also allowed to assist the healers with Magnetic Therapy (manually aligning the body's energy flow), while they worked.

I also experienced some sixty healings on my own body. It was just incredible.

The second to last day before we left Manila, I asked the healers to work on the lumps in my breast. Within thirty seconds they not only had removed two large cysts, but they also removed the scar tissue from my previous surgery. The growths actually came out of my body looking approximately the same size and shape that they felt while inside my breast.

Immediately upon my return, I visited my doctor and asked him to check the lumps again. He did so and confirmed that the cysts were no longer there. I did not have the heart to tell him what had really happened. He probably wouldn't have believed me even if I had told him.

Soon after my return, I resumed my normal activities of Psychic Counseling, Metaphysical Healing, Instructing E.S.P. Development Classes, and Coordinating Psychic Festivals.

CHAPTER 1

PSYCHIC ENERGY CENTERS
(CHAKRAS)/GROUNDING
& CLEANSING
YOUR ENERGIES/PSYCHIC PROTECTION

There are seven major psychic energy centers within the body. The upper four pertain to the development of spiritual/psychic awareness. The lower three more directly concern the physical body and materialistic drives and goals of the earth plane. These centers are commonly referred to by the Sanscrit name which is "chakras."

Each chakra rules an aspect of either the mind, the body, or the soul. They also exert an influence over the aspects of intuition, cosmic awareness and spirituality.

As cosmic energy filters into the aura, it passes through the etheric or astral body (as it is called), and finally into the chakras giving life and vitality to the physical body. As these centers become more fully vitalized their color becomes more vivid and their respective attributes of psychic ability are heightened.

CHAKRA	*COLOR*	*RULERSHIP*	*ASPECT INFLUENCED*
Crown (top of head)	Violet	Imagination	Mysticism Spiritual Devotion
Third Eye (between eyes)	Indigo	Intuition	Clairaudience Clairvoyance Intuition Visualization
Throat	Blue	Concepts	Communication Trance Mediumship
Heart	Green	Emotion	Compassion Healing Unconditional Love
Solar Plexus	Yellow	Intellect	Astral Travel Empathy Health
Spleen	Orange	Social	Filtering System for Psychic Negativity
Kundalini (base of spine)	Red	Physical	Physical Vitality Sexual Drives

GROUNDING/CLEANSING YOUR ENERGIES/ PSYCHIC PROTECTION

A technique for developing and keeping the centers clear is referred to as "grounding." This connects the cosmic or universal energies to the physical plane, through the body, as the conductor of energy. This process has a balancing or centering effect on the body, mind, and soul.

DEVELOPMENT TECHNIQUE FOR GROUNDING THE ENERGIES

Begin by sitting in a straight-back chair, with your spine straight, palms upward resting on the thighs, feet flat on the floor. Take two or three deep breaths, inhaling through the nose and exhaling through the mouth. Breathe from the diaphram for the maximum results. Visualize a silvery, white, shining light flowing freely into the top of your head. Continue imagining that the light is filling every part of your body and flowing gently down through the soles of your feet, into the center of the earth. Don't rush the process. Take as long as you need to feel and see this taking place. Don't worry if you are not able to visualize everything at first. Just believe that it is happening. The thought will be sufficient to create the energy necessary to activate the process.

NOTE: Ground and protect yourself on a daily basis, in the morning upon awakening, and before retiring for the evening. This should be done whether or not you feel the need. Eventually, the process will become automatic and the procedure will become less mechanical and very natural.

DEVELOPMENT TECHNIQUE FOR CLEANSING YOUR ENERGIES

Here is a new step you can add to the process once you have mastered the technique of being grounded. Repeat the procedure, but with each breath that you take imagine the light being pulled in; see it swirling and cleansing in a clockwise motion and moving a bit further down through each chakra as you exhale. Repeat this visualization until the light has completely filled your being. Now as the light begins to filter into the center of the earth, see it being blessed and purified with a violet flame so that no one receives the negativity that you are releasing. You see, any form of psychic toxins will be released from your auric field and psychic centers by the use of the White Light. We use the violet light to cleanse this negativity because it is considered to be the color of transmutation. As such, it has the highest, best suited vibration to change the nature of the energy, in other words, to neutralize it.

WHAT IS PSYCHIC ATTACK?

The energies from one person can mix with another person's auric field and consequently induce emotional, mental and physical responses. If the person being touched by the energy is not strong enough within their auric field to repel these influences, they will begin to produce those qualities of vibration within themselves. This is the principle upon which "psychic attack" is able to manifest. The only difference in psychic attack is that usually it is a conscious thought directed toward an individual. Conscious projection of thought is a stronger and more direct way of affecting someone's energy on any level. If those thoughts are of negative quality or intent, they can penetrate and affect a person's aura accordingly.

Many people release exceptionally strong thought transmissions during their dream state. This is because it is a time when the subconscious mind is able to express itself easily, without resistance from the conscious mind. At this time many people release such energies as hostility, fear, aggression, and anxiety, as well as the positive emotions of love, compassion, and happiness etc. If the dreamer happens to place you in his dream, under negative influences, this energy can reach out to your vibration and find you. During the night this type of "psychic attack" is more easily able to reach someone than during the day. There is not as much distraction from "static interference" or rather other energy fields to block and become interceptors and distractors for you.

In other words, if you are at work and busily occupied, chances are that you will not become receptive to a negative thought from someone because you are so busy that you don't or won't make time to be receptive to it. But at night, the situation is a little different because those distractions don't exist as heavily. That is why it is important to "protect" yourself before going to sleep.

DEVELOPMENT TECHNIQUE FOR PROTECTION

The process is simple and anyone can do it. Imagine "God's White Light" completely surrounding your auric field and body as if to create a protective dome. Firmly believe that negativity on any level cannot penetrate your psychic force field/shield. (If you don't believe in the concept of God, then call upon whatever "Divine" or "Universal" principle of energy that you easily identify with.) On a daily basis you should place yourself in a total state of protection from all forms of psychic attack and negativity.

CHAPTER 2

THE AURA

The aura reaches about two to three feet completely around the physical body, being somewhat oval or egg shape in appearance. It is composed of "prana" or pure energy. Prana filters into the soul giving life to the body. It is the spark of life that creates the consciousness of mind through our thoughts. The aura is what is referred to as a person's magnetism or charisma. This is why at times we are drawn to some people and at other times we are instantaneously repelled. However, most people don't consciously realize that it is the auric field which transmits this vibration.

Some people are naturally gifted with the ability to see auras or sense them, while others must work diligently to open the "third eye" center enough to unfold their psychic sight.

The aura is a psychic energy field that manifests its vibration in the form of color. The auric field is continuously changing in size, shape and color. It is a reflection of one's mental and emotional attitudes as well as physical state of being and is displayed through a rainbow effect of the various colored energies surrounding the physical body.

The "pranic" aura or "health" aura is visible to the untrained eye and is most easily seen about the head and shoulder area. Unlike the mental and emotional auras, the pranic aura takes on a white, or yellowish glow or a gray cast, the color depending upon the state of health of the individual. A white or yellow hue would indicate good or average health. A gray cast being indicative of poor health.

The aura's materialistic appearance is similar somewhat to that of a web of fiber-like threads or lines flowing outward from the body. If these fibers are straight, strong, and evenly spread around the body, it is a sign of good health. On the other hand, if the energy of the body is not flowing properly or if an illness is developing the fibers will appear tangled, wilted and unevenly spaced.

As a rule, grounding and running energy through the auric field and through the chakras will keep the aura nourished and strong.

THOUGHT FORMS

Positive thinking is another method of strengthening the aura. Thoughts have a very definite impact on the flow and exchange of energies within and around you. The process is similar to that of osmosis. Particles of thought filter out from the mind and merge into the aura. Then they continue to flow into the "ethers" (surrounding vibrational atmosphere). All that is needed to complete the exchange is a person whose mind is even slightly receptive to those thoughts or transmissions. They will either be accepted or rejected depending upon the strength of will and character of the party involved.

Thought forms are created by our mental activity. They vary in size, strength, and shape. Usually they appear as white spirals of energy but can also take form in the actual shape of the image visualized. Thought forms are not normally visible to the untrained eye. With practice, however, and development of the third eye, it is possible to see them.

Practice the exercises for developing and seeing the aura. This will also help you to visualize thought forms. Be patient with yourself. "Rome wasn't built in a day." Much repetition and practical application is necessary in order to become proficient with all of these techniques.

NOTE: Techniques for developing the aura will be discussed in Chapter 9.

CHAPTER 3

MEDITATION

The word meditation can mean many things. It may be to focus one's attention on an idea, an object, a noise, or movement. Or rather, the defocusing or exclusion of all these things. It may be helpful with problem solving, stress reduction, relaxation, and energy balancing. It may take the form of silent prayer or thought as a way of communicating with God and the Universe, while touching the very essence of the soul.

Meditation deals with the application of one's contemplation. It is a way of achieving self-awareness, emotional balance, and an overall feeling of harmony between oneself and the Cosmos. It is a tool for drawing in the energy needed to strengthen one's abilities in healing, psychic development, concentration, self-discipline, and cosmic awareness.

MEDITATION is the art of being, not becoming.

MEDITATION is silence.

MEDITATION is the calm of the storm.

MEDITATION is going within, rather than to direct energy externally.

MEDITATION is illumination of the soul, through the I AM presence of GOD in man.

DEVELOPMENT TECHNIQUE FOR MEDITATION

The easiest way to begin is to sit with your spine straight. The arms should be resting gently on the thighs. The legs should be straight, not crossed. Any crossing blocks the energy flow. This applies to all psychic development techniques unless otherwise specifically stated. Remember to always be sure that the spine is straight when practicing.

Begin by taking several slow, deep breaths, inhaling through the nose and exhaling through the mouth. Always breathe from the diaphram as it allows for more oxygen consumption than breathing through the lungs. It is also less stressful on the heart. Since more oxygen can circulate freely through the bloodstream, it assists in achieving a deeper state of muscle relaxation. This is why all psychic development exercises require deep breathing.

To breathe from the diaphram, feel your stomach expand as you inhale. It will contract and flatten as you exhale. Note that the shoulders do not rise up and down when you are breathing correctly. They will only rise if you are breathing from the lungs. This will enable the energy of the Universe to flow freely and easily through the psychic centers, or chakras, as they are called.

MEDITATION # 1 - REVITALIZATION

As you inhale, know that you are receiving pure energy, from the Universe to revitalize your entire being. As you exhale, imagine yourself releasing all forms of mental, physical and emotional negativity, such as tension, anxiety, illness or whatever stops you from feeling balanced in your life. Just let go and relax. Continue this for a few minutes then bring yourself back to reality feeling very rested and peaceful within.

MEDITATION # 2 - RELAXATION

Try to visualize yourself in a place you feel peaceful and serene. Let your mind ramble through some place in nature; perhaps, near a mountain or running water, like a river, in a green forest or just someplace that makes you feel good. Don't worry about restricting your thoughts. For now, just go with the flow of what is easy and comfortable to imagine. Just be an observer and don't try to control what is happening.

When you feel peaceful and relaxed, gradually begin to bring yourself back to reality. Continue the deep breathing exercises while you are bringing yourself back to full awakening consciousness. When you open your eyes, you will feel completely refreshed and very relaxed.

MEDITATION # 3 - LOVE AND ACCEPTANCE

Imagine yourself in a large spiraling, energy vortex. See it swirling in a clockwise motion around your auric field. Feel yourself becoming part of the vortex until you are able to see through to the top of it into a tunnel of love and light. It has been created by the light within and around you. Imagine that the tunnel is pink. See yourself immersed in the light of the tunnel as you begin to feel a strong sensation of love and happiness surge through your entire being. Bathe yourself with the Light of Love. Begin to radiate and project the pink light to others around you who need this feeling in their lives. It will serve to balance the emotions. When you are ready, return to the present, feeling a sensation of love and acceptance for yourself as well as others. This meditation will also serve to make you more tolerant of others' weaknesses as well as your own.

All of the development techniques in this book may be utilized as meditations. Learn to create your own meditations through visualization and affirmation. All that need be done is to visualize or imagine these things happening. When you complete the imagery of the meditation, begin to bring yourself back slowly so as to keep the sensations of the vibrations experienced within your auric field.

AFFIRMATIONS AND VISUALIZATION

AFFIRMATIONS:

An affirmation is a positive statement that declares to the Universe what you need or would like to manifest in your life. It is a way of magnetizing a thought so that it permeates the atmosphere to attract those needs and wants. Only affirm that which is for the highest and best interests of all persons concerned.

In order to manifest your desires, you must truly want them to happen. You must also believe that they are possible to attain. Above all, you must be ready and willing to accept their manifestation. If any of these conditions do not exist, achieving the things you are affirming will be difficult, if not impossible. Be realistic.

When creating affirmations, it is important to word them in the present tense. Phrase them "AS IF" they are happening exactly the way you want. Do not use negative words such as: "never," "couldn't," "wouldn't," "shouldn't," "can't," "won't," "don't," etc. Always be very positive.

Remember what Oscar Wilde once said:

"Be careful what you wish for, you MIGHT get it."

Affirmations may be read aloud or silently. They may be chanted like a mantra or written several times on a paper. Be as creative as you like.

A partial list of affirmations has been prepared as a guideline. Use it to assist you in creating your own statements.

AFFIRMATIONS

CLARITY OF PURPOSE AND WILL:

1. The Divine Light of the Universe always guides my way.
2. I am always guided by Love and Light.
3. I am an open channel for the Divine Will of God.
4. I am always guided toward my highest and best interests.

DIET:

1. I only eat when I am hungry.
2. I only eat to nourish my body.

3. I only enjoy eating foods that are nourishing and good for me.
4. I am losing (gaining) weight effortlessly.

HEALTH:

1. Every day I am feeling more radiant and healthy.
2. Every day, in every way, God is making me feel better and better.
3. The Healing Light of the Universe is filling my body with radiant health and vitality.
4. Cosmic Energy flows freely throughout my being for health and well being.
5. The healing energies of the Universe always surround me.

LOVE:

1. I am an open channel of Unconditional Love.
2. I love myself, therefore, I can love others.
3. Divine Love fills every part of my being.
4. I am always surrounded by the Love of God.
5. I am in Love with Life and the joy it brings.

PROSPERITY:

1. My needs are always more than fulfilled.
2. I always have whatever I need for my highest and best interests.
3. Prosperity and abundance in all things are coming to me now.

PROTECTION:

1. I only attract the highest, most positive energies of the universe to me.
2. Divine Love and Light surround and protect me.
3. I am completely protected by the Universal White Light.
4. The Divine Light of God is my shield.
5. I always walk in the brightest Light of the Cosmos.

RELATIONSHIPS:

1. Harmonious, loving relationships are coming to me now.
2. I only attract positive relationships.
3. The perfect mate is coming to me now. We are perfect for each other in every way.
4. I always attract well-balanced, meaningful relationships in my life.
5. Relationships only come to me if they are for my highest and best interests.

SELF-ESTEEM:

1. I completely accept myself for who and what I am. I am totally accepted by others.
2. There is substance and reason in my being. I am a part of the Divine Plan of the Universe.
3. I deserve the good things that life has to offer.
   They are coming to me now.

VISUALIZATION

Visualization is the process of seeing mental pictures and images. It is a way of affirming and manifesting your desires. The experience is similar to that of daydreaming. The area of the body that works in affinity with visual ability is located between the eyes. This is referred to as the "third eye." It is the aspect of sight that is utilized while we dream.

The first step to manifest something is through thought. When we think of something we mentally create a visual form. The intensity of that thought along with the clarity of its visual image permeates the atmosphere. It then has the ability to attract other energies of the same nature back to the point of origin. That point is you. You do not need to believe in metaphysical practices or spiritual concepts in order to manifest your desire. However, you must believe that your mind has the power to create your goal. It is necessary to remain very positive in your outlook about the outcome. In addition to thinking positively, one must physically do as much as possible to help their wishes manifest.

DEVELOPMENT TECHNIQUE FOR LEARNING TO VISUALIZE

To strengthen the ability to visualize one may stare with both eyes for about one minute at an area where there are few objects. It may be any type of setting. The next step is to close the eyes and try to remember and visualize the objects exactly as they are placed as well as their exact appearance. When this has been done, look back at the area to determine the accuracy of the visualization. This technique may be repeated as often as necessary to achieve the desired result. It is suggested that you practice no longer than ten minutes per sitting.

DEVELOPMENT TECHNIQUE FOR VISUALIZING A GOAL

First decide what your goals are. Then visualize or imagine that the conditions to obtain your desires already exist. Then, in your mind's eye, see or feel them happening in the present, exactly as you want them to be.

Don't worry if you have difficulty in visualizing the picture or scene. What is important to do is to firmly believe or feel that the concept is really forming, whether you can see it or not. Simply imagine that what you want is and so it will be. Remember, the power of thought is very strong and is equally effective as the power of visualization. In time, your abilities to imagine and visualize will develop.

Focus your energy on your goals often, but do not allow yourself to become obsessed with them. Excessive energy releases a feeling of anxiety into the ethers. Anxiety only exists when one is expecting something to happen. The basis of your visualization is in seeing your goals as if they already exist, exactly the way that you want them to be.

CHAPTER 4

METAPHYSICAL HEALING

To heal means to "make whole or stable" by restoring health to the mental, emotional, and physical bodies. There are a variety of ways in which to conduct a healing. Among them are:

1. Absentee Healing by Mental Projection of Healing Energies and Thoughts
2. Aura Cleansing
3. Chakra Balancing
4. Color Breathing
5. Energy-Charged Water
6. Gemstone Therapy
7. Magnetic Therapy
8. Magnetized Cloth

While there are many types of healings, there are certain conditions which must always be met in order to effect a proper treatment.

1. The patient must truly want to be healed.
2. He must be ready to search out the cause of his illness.
3. He must be able to release the cause or it could manifest again in the future and create the same illness.

WHAT CAUSES ILLNESS?

It is important to note that illness can be the result of a past life which has not yet been released. It can be a Karmic Debt or a lesson needed for spiritual growth and development.

If the pranic energies of the aura are allowed to become depleted, it creates a corresonding depletion of energy in the chakras and eventually physical, mental, or emotional illness or imbalance.

Depletion of the pranic energies generally occurs through abnormally long work hours, lack of rest and relaxation, deprivation of social influences for enjoyment, improper eating habits, use or consumption of mind-altering substances such as alcohol, caffeine, tobacco, narcotics (both prescription and non-prescription drugs), etc. Moderation is the key word here for improvement of the health.

RESTORING THE PHYSICAL, MENTAL, AND SPIRITUAL BODIES TO HEALTH

Restoration may be accomplished in two ways:
1. Revitalizing the auric field through Color Breathing
2. Through polarity balancing of the chakras with Magnetic Therapy

In addition, should an illness or phobia be the result of a Karmic situation, it may be resolved by going through a Past Life Regression. This is usually done while in a state of hypnosis for the maximum effect. Once the patient discovers the origin of the problem, he is made to see that he no longer needs to hold on to it as the experience pertains only to the past and serves no purpose in the present. Once this is accepted and recognized it can be released.

If an illness has resulted as a manifestation of mental or emotional imbalance, it may be further corrected through the externalization of one's feelings, thoughts, and desires. The feelings, thoughts, and desires must also be brought into proper perspective through a logical and realistic approach to confronting and dealing with the matter at hand. This is when psychological counseling and therapy may be of considerable value in determining and releasing the cause of the problem.

Remember, if the cause is not completely released, it may inhibit or totally block the cure. Temporary relief of the condition might be achieved. However, the symptoms could manifest again at a later time.

LEGALITIES OF PERFORMING A HEALING

The following criteria have been established by most professional healers in order to protect oneself from the possibility of legal implications arising from the conditions of performing a healing:

1. The healer must never diagnose or prescribe unless he is a licensed, certified medical doctor, whose practice is in the state in which the healing is being performed.

2. The healer must never slide or vibrate his hand while touching the patient's body unless he has a certified license for massage therapy in the state in which he is conducting the healing.
3. The healer must never claim that the patient will be cured.
4. The healer must always wash his hands before giving a treatment in order to comply with health regulations.
5. The healer must always obtain the patient's permission to perform a treatment.

OBTAINING PERMISSION TO HEAL

If the patient is present, try to obtain permission in writing. A written agreement will not necessarily protect you from legal implication. However, it will serve to establish the patient's willingness to try this method of healing.

On the agreement, state plainly that you are not a medical doctor and as such, are practicing holistic/metaphysical techniques of healing. Make no claims as to the ability of the healing to effect a cure.

If you are doing an absentee healing (a healing that takes place without the patient being physically present), you must intuitively obtain permission to go ahead.

DEVELOPMENT TECHNIQUE FOR OBTAINING PERMISSION INTUITIVELY

To obtain permission intuitively, go into a meditative or quiet state of being. Try to make mental contact with the patient and ask if they desire a healing. If the response seems positive then continue to inform the patient that he must also be willing to release the cause of the illness, no matter what it is. Otherwise, it could return again.

It may be helpful for visualization in this technique if you are provided with a photo of the patient. It is also good to know his name, as you can tune in vibrationally to him (through its sound) regardless of his geographical location. The steps to follow are the same as outlined in the Healing Check List. The only exception is that you are mentally visualizing doing the healing since it is by the absentee method.

Explain that you will help him to determine the cause and then to let go of it. At this point, again ask if he still wishes to be healed. If you feel that the answer is yes, then continue. If there is any doubt, simply send him White Light. Project it with your mind and see it completely around his auric field. If you see that he absorbs the light, he has accepted the healing and you may proceed with your healing technique. If you still are unable to determine what is happening, don't worry. He will only absorb energy if he needs and wants it. Understand that the White Light cannot give off a negative effect, so you cannot hurt him with the energy. All you can do is help. Under these circumstances, not being sure of his desire, you should stop the healing at this point. Don't worry if you experience difficulty in knowing or feeling if the patient wishes to be healed. In time, with practice, you will develop a natural feel for visualizing and sensing.

MAGNETIC THERAPY

Magnetic Therapy utilizes polarity balancing to restore the body's natural magnetic alignment. It is also referred to as energy balancing. This method is able to remove blockages of energy so that prana flows freely through the body and its energy centers as well as the auric field.

1. Energy flows from negative to positive in order to create a current. Some healers prefer not to touch the patient when they transfer energy. Others lay their hands directly on the surface to be treated. The choice is yours as it is merely a matter of preference.

2. The hands are capable of establishing an electro-magnetic current of energy throughout the body.

3. Once the energy is properly flowing the body can begin to heal itself.

To insure that the vital energies will be properly transferred, both the healer and the patient should remove all metal. Metal is a strong conductor of energy and tends to distract or disrupt the flow of magnetism. Materials such as wool and leather, which insulate, should also be avoided as they also interfere with the proper transference of energies.

It is recommended to have the patient lie on a massage table. If one is not available then a low-back or no-back chair may be used. Try to use a chair which is constructed with material other than metal, for the reason stated above. If you have no other choice than to use a metal chair, then at least minimize its negative effect by placing a cushion on the seat and instruct the patient not to lean against any of the metal parts. It also helps to place a wool (real wool, not synthetic) blanket on the seat, against the back, and have the patient place his feet on it. This insulates him. The last alternative would be to have the patient stand during the treatment. In any case, make sure that you are able to easily access all areas requiring treatment.

Since the healer is the means for transferring health and vitality to the patient, it is essential that he be in good health when conducting a treatment. While the healer is not using his own vital magnetism to heal, he is drawing upon the cosmic energies of the universe to filter through him as a conductor of energy, to complete a circuit between himself and the patient. However, since the energies passing from him will contain particles of his auric field, he must be be in good health to effect a proper healing. The healer must always clear his own magnetism before working with a patient. To do this involves grounding his energies and placing himself in a complete state of protection by surrounding himself with the "White Light." He should also cleanse his auric field before and after each session. Since the hands are used to remove impurities in the energy of the patient, they should be washed in cold water immediately after treatment to remove any particles of negativity that remain.

POLARITY OF THE BODY

The front of the body is positive and the back is of negative polarity. The top of the head is positive, the mid-section is neutral and from that point down to the area of the feet is of negative polarity.

TECHNIQUE FOR DETERMINING
THE POLARITY OF THE HANDS

The true test for proving which of the hands is positive and which is negative is established by determining right- or left-eye dominance. If you are right-eye dominant, your right hand is of positive polarity and your left hand will be negative. If you are left-eye dominant, your left hand is of positive polarity and your right hand is negative.

To take this test, obtain a piece of paper, large enough to cover your face. Place a hole in the center of the paper no larger than the tip of a pencil eraser. Hold the paper with both hands, directly in front of your face, with both arms extended. Focus through the hole with both eyes, on an object that is about 15 feet away from you. Very slowly bring the paper toward your face until it touches your nose. Notice which eye is still looking through the hole. That is your dominant eye.

Many people believe that right- or left-handedness is the determining factor for dominance. In some cases it may apply. However, there are times when it does not. For instance, a child in school may have had their writing hand changed over by the teacher. Another case would be when one sustains an injury such as a broken finger. In order to compensate, the other hand is used for all activities. It then assumes the role of the dominant hand.

There are many times when right- or left-handedness corresponds to right- or left-eye dominance. However, to be sure of your polarity, check to see which eye is dominant.

DEVELOPMENT TECHNIQUE FOR CREATING AN ENERGY CURRENT

First, the healer needs to get his energies flowing through his hands. To do this he should briskly rub the palms of his hands together. Next, to establish a current within the patient, it is necessary for the healer to place his positive hand on a positive polarity area of the body and his negative hand on the corresponding negative polarity part or the area to be treated. Now visualize a current of energy flowing between your hands, through the patient.

If the patient expresses a sensation of discomfort check to be sure that your polarity matches his. This procedure will not put in or take out energy. It will simply realign and establish the proper magnetic flow. Once the energies have been opened, the area being treated will begin to pulsate. This is the signal that the circuit has been completed and that the healer has accomplished his goal. He may then remove his hands from the recipient. As a rule you should not use this procedure for longer than ten minutes on each area requiring treatment. Follow-up sessions may be repeated after a 24-hour period if necessary.

PUTTING IN ENERGY

The positive hand is used for putting in energy, as it is naturally charged for sending by virtue of the body's magnetic alignment. This method is best used in cases of energy depletion to restore vitality to the body. It is also useful in cases when drawing out could be painful, since putting in generally produces no more than a tingling sensation of warmth.

DEVELOPMENT TECHNIQUE FOR PUTTING IN ENERGY

Begin by briskly rubbing the hands together with the palms facing each other. This creates an immediate flow of energy between the hands. Place the positive hand, palm down, over the area to be treated. Extend the negative arm toward the sky, with the palm upward while holding the hand slightly cupped. This position allows the energy to be drawn into the negative hand from the universe. It is then channeled through the arm to the positive hand and into the patient. While you are putting in the energy, you may also wish to send a particular color to aid in the revitalization of the patient's energies. Maintain this position until the transference has been completed. This process usually takes from three to five minutes.

DRAWING OUT ENERGY

The negative hand is used for drawing out any impurities or blockages of energy that may impede the life-force energies of the body. Once the natural magnetism of the body is restored, it allows new vitality to permeate every organ, thereby allowing the body to restore itself to radiant health.

While one is drawing out energy, it may create a feeling of slight pressure or a throbbing effect within the patient. It also tends to produce a pulling effect very similar to that of Epsom Salt when it is drawing out an infection. Sometimes the patient will continue to feel this effect of pulling for a day or so. This is quite natural and is not something to worry about.

Since this process may create slight discomfort for the patient, make sure to ask them to tell you what sensations they are experiencing. Do not, however, program their subconscious mind by telling them exactly what to expect. Some people are extremely sensitive to suggestion. Forewarning them of a possible occurence is likely to produce it. If drawing out becomes too uncomfortable for the patient try creating a circuit of energy with both hands or simply put in energy with the positive hand.

DEVELOPMENT TECHNIQUE FOR DRAWING OUT ENERGY

Begin by briskly rubbing the palms together in order to create a current between them. To draw out energy, the negative hand should be open with the palm facing directly on or over the area to be treated. Extend the positive arm with the hand open and the palm facing the earth. Now visualize all negative energy or blockages being drawn into your negative hand and flowing through to your positive hand where it will filter into the earth. As the current flows out of the positive hand, visualize or imagine that it is being purified with a violet flame so as to disintegrate all negative vibrations.

With practice, the healer will become aware of when to stop drawing out energy. As his own magnetism increases, he will become more sensitive to the pulling sensation that this process creates. A general indicator of completion is when the energy seems to stop flowing as if the connection were broken. There will also be an accompanying feeling of coolness in the negative hand. As a rule, the process of drawing out takes from three to five minutes to complete.

If you put in energy after opening the body's channels it can be most effective in restoring the body's magnetism. However, as always, make sure to clear the magnetism of your hands by shaking them off before transferring new energy to the patient.

Never draw out energy from the heart or solar plexus as these are the vital centers which enable the body to sustain life-force. In these areas it is best to use the technique of "Creating an Energy Current." This is sufficient to keep the energies clear and flowing.

DEVELOPMENT TECHNIQUE FOR INTENSIFYING THE ENERGY

This method may be applied for either putting in or taking out energy. This may be done by placing the back sides of both hands together. The palm side should not touch either hand. To "put in," place the positive hand on the area to be healed, then place the back side of the negative hand on top of the back side of the positive hand. To "draw out," reverse the position of the hands. While this is being done it may be helpful to visualize seeing the energy flowing in or out depending on your purpose. Again, when drawing out, visualize the energy flowing out of your palm into the ethers and being purified by a violet flame.

CLEANSING THE AURA

When there are blockages of energy in the aura, the resulting effect may be physical or emotional imbalance, which could manifest in some form of illness. Usually the illness will correspond to the general area of the blockage and will also relate to the chakra or energy center nearest that location. By cleansing and strengthening the aura, the physical body is aided in its restoration to health and vitality.

DEVELOPMENT TECHNIQUE FOR CLEANSING THE AURA

Hold the hands slightly cupped with the thumbs lightly touching. The palms should be facing the patient. Starting from just above the head, make a slow, steady, sweeping motion toward the earth. This should take about 20 or 30 seconds. As the hands reach the floor, shake them off to clear any negative energy. Shake them as if you were trying to throw off water from them. To be effective the movement should be slightly abrupt. Then, with the hands closed into a fist, raise them again above the head. Open the hands and repeat the procedure until the entire auric field has been cleared.

NOTE: Raising an open hand, palm facing the body, from the negative pole of the body to the positive pole will tend to stimulate or open the chakra centers. The same motion, downward from the head to the feet will close the energy centers. The hands are closed into fists before raising them so as to avoid confusing the body's magnetic flow.

DEVELOPMENT TECHNIQUE FOR COLOR BREATHING

The aura may be strengthened through a process known as "Color Breathing." To do this, simply place yourself in a meditative or relaxed state of mind and breathe deeply and slowly from the diaphram. Inhale through the nose and exhale through the mouth. Imagine and try to visualize each breath permeating and filling your auric field. See each of the colors of the chakras filtering in, one at a time. Remember, you will automatically absorb the colors that your aura needs. Any excess energy will be passed off into the ethers or spiritual planes of vibration. If you experience difficulty in visualizing the colors, don't worry. It will come in time, with practice. For now, just believe that it is happening. You will still receive the desired benefit and effect.

ENERGY-CHARGED WATER

The consumption of energy-charged water is another way of replenishing the vital energies of the body. This method is most beneficial when used in conjunction with Magnetic Therapy. Immediately following a treatment, give the patient 6 ounces of charged water to drink. Instruct them to continue drinking small doses of the water for three days. You may magnetize it for them. They should consume 4 ounces every three hours during the day as well as 4 ounces just prior to retiring for the evening.

Energy-charged water is also beneficial to drink any time you feel the need for a "pick-me-up." It will help to revitalize your energies almost immediately.

DEVELOPMENT TECHNIQUE FOR ENERGY-CHARGING WATER

Begin by briskly rubbing the palms of your hands together to get the energy flowing through your hands. Take a cool glass of tap water and hold it in the hand of negative polarity. Place the positive hand with the palm side directly over the opening. You do not need to actually touch the water. Begin to mentally project healing thoughts, color, and energy. Take as long as you need to complete the transfer of magnetism. This process generally takes from three to five minutes.

NOTE: Make sure to only use tap water. De-ionized water does not have the capability of transferring energy. Tap water has both negative and positive ions. This is what enables the energy to saturate the water with its healing vibration.

If you feel the need of a particular color to be used for the healing, you can put a few drops of food coloring into the water before charging. You need to experiment with this in order to get the color you want.

MAGNETIZED CLOTH

A cloth may be magnetized for transmitting healing energy. This is an excellent tool for absentee healing. It should be worn by the patient over the area in need of treatment. If it is not possible to wear the cloth, it should be worn or carried as close to the person as possible in order to transfer its magnetism.

No one except the recipient should be allowed to handle or use the cloth as it has been specifically magnetized to meet the patient's needs.

DEVELOPMENT TECHNIQUE FOR MAGNETIZED CLOTH

Prepare a plain white or colored piece of cotton or flannel cloth large enough to cover the area being treated. Refer to the color chart to determine the proper color to use. Briskly rub the palms together to create a flow of magnetism between the hands. Place the cloth between the palms. Mentally project whatever healing thoughts, color, and energies that may be helpful in restoring the patient to health and vitality.

NOTE: The cloth should not be made of synthetic materials, wool, or leather. These fabrics are best used wrapping the cloth when preparing it for mailing to the patient. Since these materials do not transfer energy they serve as a protective shield (insulator) from vibrations which could change the magnetism of the cloth.

GEMSTONE THERAPY

A variety of gemstones may be used for healing. They may be purchased at a lapidary store. Remember, however, that they work through the auric field of an individual to affect various aspects of the mental, emotional, and physical bodies.

CARING FOR YOUR GEMSTONES:

Always clear the energy of your stones after using them for any type of healing. It is important to cleanse any newly acquired gems as you have no idea of what energies they might contain. This is best done by placing them in warm salt water for a minimum of 3 hours. Use about 3 Tbsp. to 8 ounces of water. Warm water is used with salt to activate its chemical structure so as to affect its drawing power. In actuality, cold tends to be a stronger cleansing agent than heat. If salt is unavailable, place them in as cold water as possible, also for a couple of hours.

After you have cleared them, it is preferable to store your healing stones and generator, in a leather or wool pouch to insulate them from other energies. In this manner, they will always be ready to use at a moment's notice. They can also be placed in a wooden box. Wood is a neutral insulator.

There are also times when it is best not to clear the vibrations from your stones, as in the case of trying to build the energy with your own magnetism for meditative purposes. The stronger the vibration, the more it will enhance your efforts.

All types of energy generators should be allowed to build and retain their magnetism. There is no need to cleanse them as they are only to be used for storing and transferring energy to other stones which will do the actual healing. Of course, even generators must be cleared when first acquired.

GETTING ACQUAINTED WITH YOUR STONES:

Begin by clearing the energies in your stones by placing them in warm salt water for about three hours. Rinse them off in cold water and dry them. One at a time, hold each stone in your receiving or negative polarity hand. Carefully study the markings of each stone. While doing a meditation with each stone, feel yourself merging into it and becoming one with its energy. Become totally aware and sensitive to the feel of its healing qualities. When you have finished your meditation, record any thoughts and feelings that you have received about its usefulness as a healing tool.

Stones react differently for different people. There is no set way of knowing which stone will produce a desired effect. Eventually, you will be able to determine which gemstones seem to work in affinity with your healing abilities. This is all a matter of sensitivity and preference.

If ever you feel uncomfortable in handling any stone, it is a definite sign that you should avoid working with it. It simply means that it does not blend with your vibratory field. If you wish, you can try the stone again at a later time and see if you feel differently or the same. If you feel the same it is probably better for you to forget about that particular stone. However, if you feel alright about it when you try it at a later time, then the energies are probably compatible and it would be O.K. to work with it. Let your own feeling be your guide and you will probably be correct. After all, there is no set rule for choosing stones. Some metaphysicians say that the stones choose you.

Another method of determining which stones to use for healing is through the use of the pendulum. (NOTE: The subject of making and using a pendulum is discussed more completely in Chapter 9.) To do this, place the stones, one at a time, on a flat surface which is non-conductive such as wood or rubber. A sink mat or bath mat is a good source for this. Ask the pendulum if the stone is good for you to use for yourself.

When the patient is present, place the stones you plan to use in his negative polarity hand, one at a time, with the palm open. Hold the pendulum over his hand while asking if that stone will be good to work with for that person.

You will find that while some stones are in affinity with your own personal magnetism, they will not respond for treatment of certain individuals. Also, some stones will work for everyone and some stones will work for only one individual you treat and not for others.

WORKING WITH QUARTZ CRYSTALS:

To date, the most effective known gemstone is the quartz crystal. The energy principle of quartz is similar to that of the pyramids in terms of its magnetic capabilities. Because of its inherent ability as a transmitter and receiver, it is extremely valuable in sending and receiving healing thoughts and energies. The old-time crystal radio sets were made with quartz crystals. Quartz crystal may also be used as a generator to energize other stones and objects so that they may be readily usable for their specific purpose.

Clear quartz is reputed to be best suited for polarization of the body's magnetic alignment; whereas amethyst quartz is claimed to be best for healing, due to its color. The vibratory rate of violet is such that it can create structural changes in matter. It is often referred to as the "Ray of Transmutation" or change. Either type of crystal will be very effective for transferring or accumulating energy.

LEAD CRYSTALS:

Unlike the natural formation of gemstones, lead crystal is man-made. It is composed of sand and lead. As such, its magnetic capabilities are deadened since its structural quality is extremely dense. Consequently, it has no potential for amplifying or transferring energy. Consider the manner in which radioactive material is disposed of — IN A SOLID LEAD CAPSULE! For this reason it is imperative not to use or store lead crystal with gemstones. Even the proximity of lead crystal could lessen their effectiveness because of its gross properties. MOST ESPECIALLY IT SHOULD NOT BE WORN ON THE PERSON.

SELECTING A CRYSTAL:

When determining which crystal to buy, there are a few things to check for. First, the stone should be very clear. The less fracturing or inclusions in its makeup the better. Clear stones can more easily accumulate and transfer the energies. If the stone is going to be held in the hand, make sure it has a large, flat edge that will rest comfortably against the palm. The flat edge should be part of the pointed end. If a colored quartz is desired, make sure that its color is deep and translucent. It is preferable to select a crystal with one pointed end. Energy will flow into the gem through the rough, unfinished end and will then be directed as necessary through the point.

When selecting a crystal as an energy generator it is best to use clear quartz, the reason being that the clear color allows for better adaptability in creating different types of energy fields. It should be at least four or five inches in length and about two and a half to three inches thick. If a larger crystal is desired, it may be used. However, it should be stored away, in an insulated material, such as wood, when not in use. The larger the crystal, the more energy it will generate. Some of the energy could be so intense as to induce feelings of anxiety or nervousness and even minor headaches. This only happens when the individual working with those crystals is not developed enough to properly channel those energies in his auric field.

ACTIVATING YOUR GENERATOR CRYSTAL:

First, make sure that you have cleared its energy with the salt water solution. You may then follow any of the procedures listed here to activate and energize your generator:

1. Place your crystal in direct sunlight for several hours to activate it by the absorption of solar energy. This is the easiest method to use. The natural power of the sun is quite strong and is one of the best sources of energy for utilization.

2. Another way of activating the magnetic properties of your generator crystal is to place the pointed or positive end to the north, and set a magnet underneath the south end. This will start the energy flowing into the south, or negative end, and then into the north, or positive end. Energy flows from negative to positive, in order to create a current.

3. Still another method involves the use of pyramid energy. Place your crystal directly underneath the apex of any frame or model of the "Great Pyramid of Giza." This

may also be accomplished by placing the crystal on top of what is called a "pyramid energy grid." This is a metal plate shaped into several miniature pyramids which contains a magnet inside of it for activating the energies. Pyramid structures can usually be found in metaphysical book stores.

4. One may also activate a crystal by using his own vibratory or magnetic field as a stimulus. This is done by holding the crystal in the negative hand and consciously directing energy into it by mental projection. The point of the gem should be facing north. This is most easily accomplished while in a meditative state.

USING YOUR GENERATOR CRYSTAL TO ENERGIZE GEMSTONES:

Please note that all of the methods of activating the generator crystal may be used for energizing other gemstones. However, it is recommended to use the generator, as it will greatly enhance the natural capabilities of other stones. Since crystal has the power to transfer energy without distortion, it is an excellent tool for charging the energies of even the densest stone, which might not be possible by any other method. It can't, however, be used with lead crystal.

ADDITIONAL SUGGESTIONS
FOR CHARGING GEMSTONES

PROCEDURE:

Gemstones may be charged by placing them in a container of cool tap water. Make sure to never use distilled or de-ionized water, since it will not transfer vibrations. Always make sure that stones are cleansed before placing them in water. The water should at least cover them. The container and stones should then be left in bright sunlight for several hours. The sun will not only charge the stones, but will also energize the water, which will be permeated with the gems' magnetism. WARNING: Some stones can create toxins in water and this water should never be taken orally. Quartz crystals, however, are non-toxic and the water used to charge them may be used as a spiritual bath for healing, or may be drunk as a tonic. A most effective drink mixture is made from water charged with clear quartz crystals. After charging the water, make sure to remove all stones, as they should not be consumed.

PROCEDURE:

Individual stones may be energized by placing them around a crystal generator, in a circle. Make sure that the point of the crystal generator is facing north. This will assist in creating the proper magnetic flow. If you are not certain which way is north, it is better to use a compass. Charge the stones for a few hours, and then store them away for future use. Place them in an insulated pouch, such as leather or wool.

DEVELOPMENT TECHNIQUE FOR POLARITY BALANCING

Have the recipient lie down while holding two clear quartz crystals. One should be in each hand. The pointed edge should be facing flat against the negative palm, pointing toward the wrist. The other point in the positive hand should be palm down, facing away from the body. This will create a flow of energy within the body. In order to close the circuit, the healer should also place his negative palm over the bottom of the patient's negative foot, and the positive palm over the bottom of the positive foot. This way, the healer is able to consciously direct the flow of energy by aligning the current to run from negative to positive. It is also a good visualization to instruct the recipient to imagine energy flowing in a circle through his body from the negative side to the positive. He should see it continue to flow freely through himself over and over until the process is completed. This should take about three to five minutes. Again, as with Magnetic Healing, the healer's hands will become noticeably cool when the energies are flowing properly, and in sufficient quantity. This will signal the close of the treatment.

DEVELOPMENT TECHNIQUE FOR BALANCING THE CHAKRAS USING THE PENDULUM

A pendulum may be used for this technique. (NOTE: The subject of making and using a pendulum is discussed more completely in Chapter 9.) Have the patient lie down on his back. One at a time, check to see if the chakra is open, by holding the pendulum directly over it. Some people's energy fields are stronger than others. Start by holding the pendulum a few inches above the chakra, and continue to lower it gradually until you locate its energy field. In some cases, the energy force of the chakra will create a more powerful gyration of the pendulum. Since your position is reversed to the person, the pendulum should move in a counterclockwise motion if the energy is flowing properly through the chakra. This would indicate that the polarity of the chakra is "positive." If the pendulum moves in a clockwise motion, it is an indication that the energy flowing through the chakra is of excessive "negative" polarity and should be corrected. If the pendulum moves in a diagonal direction instead of a circular motion, it is an indication that there is a blockage of energy which must be cleared.

SHUTTING-DOWN OR SLOWING THE ENERGY OF THE CHAKRAS

There are times when it would be desirable to "shut-down" the energy of the chakras, as in the case of a healing. However, make sure to check the polarity of the chakras before doing this. This should be done while the patient is lying down on his back. Cup your negative hand very slightly. Start from the area just above the top of the head and make a slow, steady, downward, sweeping motion to just beyond the feet. As you do this, mentally direct the energy of the chakras to close. You may also have the patient help you by imagining the petals of a large flower closing in each chakra. Once the centers are closed, the healer can more effectively re-establish the proper flow or polarity of energy in the chakra being treated. At this point, the healer should again check the polarity of the chakras with the pendulum to be sure that the treatment has been effective. After the treatment has been completed, open the chakras by running your positive hand upward from the feet to just above the head, while mentally willing the centers to open. If you forget to re-open all of the centers, don't worry. They will automatically open within a few minutes on their own.

NOTE: It might also be helpful to "slow" the energy of a particular chakra, as in the case of an overactive thyroid gland (throat center), or a heart condition of high blood pressure (heart center). This may be done by either the patient or the healer. Using the negative hand, direct the chakra to slow down, not close, its activity, by making a counterclockwise motion over the chakra (when done by the patient). If this is done by the healer, he will make a clockwise motion with his hand, because of reversed polarity.

CORRECTING EXCESSIVE NEGATIVE ENERGY

When there is an excess of negative energy in the chakra, the result is that of depleting the energy to a point of its eventually closing down altogether. To correct this, take the patient through the "polarity balancing" technique on page   . When finished, take the crystal out of his negative hand and put the colored stone to be used for the corresponding chakra in place of it. Leave the remaining crystal in his positive hand, and place that hand directly over the center being treated. This will give a charge of positive energy to the center. Now complete the "polarity circuit" again by holding your positive palm directly over the bottom of the positive foot, and the negative palm directly over the bottom of the negative foot. In this manner, you may mentally direct the energy to flow into the chakra. The entire process should require no more than three minutes for each chakra treated. This method may also be used on oneself. The only variation requires closing the energies of the circuit by sitting in a lotus position.

CORRECTING BLOCKAGES OF ENERGY

To correct a blockage of energy in a chakra, create a circuit of energy. To do this, have the patient lie down on his back. After briskly rubbing the hands together, the healer places his positive hand directly over or on the chakra being treated, on the front (positive polarity side) of the patient. The healer then places his negative hand directly over or on the same location, on the back (negative polarity side) of the patient. At this point, the healer may also mentally will the energy to flow from negative to positive within the chakra. This will give the process an added boost. When the current has been established, the healer's hands will become noticeably cool. This will signal the close of the treatment. This method usually takes about three minutes per chakra.

QUARTZ CRYSTAL AS JEWELRY

Quartz crystals may be worn as jewelry, but take care to wear them correctly. (Don't wear lead crystal). If worn as a ring, the point, if there is one, should be facing you. This will bring in energy. It should be worn on the receiving or negative hand. In the case of sending energy, it may be worn on the positive hand, with the point facing outward. If wearing a smooth, polished stone, it should be made to touch the skin under the setting. The setting should be made of gold or silver to insure the best conducting of energy. However, grosser metals may be used, but do not use lead. A type of jewelry is made from something called "pot-metal." This should not be worn as it has a large lead content.

Copper is a very high conductor and can be used with success in most cases. However, there are people who are allergic to copper, as well as other metals. If you have any breaking out of the skin where you are wearing any metal jewelry, change the setting to another metal. Very few people are allergic to gold, but many seem to have a reaction to silver and turn it black. You will have to do some experimenting to find out the best metal for you to wear as jewelry.

If worn as a pendant or tie tack, the point should be facing toward the earth. This will create a grounding effect in your energies. If worn with the point facing the sky, it will be useful for meditative or spiritual purposes. However, be careful not to wear the point up during normal daily activities. It could tend to make you a little dreamy or mentally "not with it" in the materiality of the earth plane.

Some pendants are even available with two points, one up and one down. This is good to create a stronger sense of balance between the spiritual energies and the material world.

QUARTZ CRYSTAL DECOR

Place a piece of quartz crystal, approximately three to four inches in size in various locations throughout the home or business. Since crystals transfer thought forms, you may easily utilize this trait by placing different types of quartz in rooms of corresponding energy.

For instance, in a weight training area of a health club a piece of clear quartz would help to strengthen the vibration of physical energy and promote a feeling of trying harder to maintain one's personal appearance. Be careful, however, as certain individuals may tend to lower the integrity of the energy by being extremely negative. This too, can be worked with by frequently clearing the energy of the crystal and mentally fortifying its intent through thought projection. Eventually the energy field will clear and even the most negative person will become positive and enthusiastic.

This method can be very therapeutic in revitalizing the body. Place an amethyst quartz in an area where healing work is performed, such as massage therapy, rebirthing, metaphysical healing, etc. It does best in a positive and relaxed environment.

It may also be useful if placed in an area where much time is spent in mental deliberation. The crystals will magnify the power of the mind and help to add an energy boost so that one feels less drained or fatigued from strong mental effort.

Concentrate your desires into them and they will manifest through the power of crystal amplification.

HEALING CHECK LIST

Follow this procedure in the sequence listed:

1. Obtain permission to do the healing, either written or oral.
2. Both the healer and the patient should remove all metal and loosen any constrictive clothing.
3. Cleanse your own aura.
4. Wash your hands with cold water.
5. Ground and protect yourself.
6. Cleanse the patient's aura.
7. Use magnetic therapy to balance the polarity.
   If you are going to use healing stones, have the patient hold them while you balance the energy. This is also

the time to use the healing cloth or to have the patient do color breathing or meditation.

8. Seal and protect the patient's aura.

9. Give him a glass of color-charged water to drink.

10. As he stands, caution him to do so slowly as he could become dizzy.

11. Cleanse your aura. Then, wash your hands with cold water to clear any negative energies.

12. Instruct your client to go home and rest for at least an hour, or as long as possible, to let the energy settle so that the healing may be effective.

13. Instruct your client to return in 72 hours if the condition persists, or if you feel that it might require follow uptreatment.

NOTE: Do not repeat a healing of this intensity before 72 hours have passed, as you would be giving the patient more energy than he could utilize. Even though the excess energy would cast itself off from the aura and body, it could still produce excess negative energy. This could temporarily result in extreme anxiety or nervousness.

COLOR CHART FOR HEALING

The mental, emotional, and physical bodies strongly respond to color therapy. Each color has unique qualities and capabilities for maintaining and restoring the body's vital life-giving forces. Through the mental projection of color, the body is able to absorb the healing energies needed to restore vitality. This chart shows various applications.

BLUE:

This is a color that must be used with care. While it is able to instill a feeling of peace, harmony, and tranquillity it is also capable of creating moodiness or depression. BLUE should never be used for persons who are sad, depressed, or manic-depressive. Another aspect of BLUE is its anesthetic and antiseptic qualities. It may also be used to create coolness. BLUE may be used to open aspects of communication between yourself and others. It also helps to insure restful sleep.

BROWN & EARTH TONES:

These colors represent the earth. Therefore, they may be used for matters dealing with "grounding the energies," neutrality, and material possessions.

GREEN:

This color produces a stimulating and revitalizing effect on the nervous system and should also be used with care when dealing with the heart and circulatory system. DARK GREEN would be used to elevate the blood pressure. However, when working with high blood pressure or heart patients, a mild shade such as AVOCADO GREEN is most effective and beneficial. GREEN may also be used to produce a cooling and soothing effect. It is the ray that The Master Jesus worked through, as a healer, while on the earth plane. Other properties of this color are utilized for financial prosperity, luck, and fertility.

INDIGO:

This color works in affinity with the mind and nervous system. A combination of blue and violet, it intensifies the qualities of both and is most effective in dealing with disorders such as hyperactivity, obsession, insomnia, extreme tension, stress, and anxiety. When mentally projected, this color can help to expel negative thoughts and desires.

ORANGE:

This color aids assimilation and digestion and may be useful in cases involving the circulatory system when red cannot be used. This gentle ray of energy works in affinity with the lungs, throat and chest.

RED:

This color has a strong stimulating and revitalizing effect on the nervous system and the blood and should be used with care when dealing with matters of the heart and circulatory system. It may be useful in helping to raise the blood pressure but should be used with caution on heart patients or persons with high blood pressure. (It is recommended that ORANGE be substituted for RED in that case). RED may be used well in cases of blood deficiencies, such as anemia. It is also beneficial in providing a feeling of warmth or heat.

ROSE-PINK:

This is a mixture of WHITE and RED (Truth, Purity and the Passion of Love) and brings to light the true concept of unconditional selfless love, without sexual connotations. If utilized properly, it will help one to become a more loving and accepting person, as well as to feel that they are more loved by others. It is called the ray of Unconditional Love.

VIOLET:

This color is the symbol of power and will serve as an aid in helping one to gain control over the various aspects in his life. It is used to enhance the imagination in matters of creative reasoning. When used for purification, it is most effective. One of its strongest properties is transmutation, the ability to create change. It gives restful sleep.

WHITE:

This is the all-purpose color that may be designated for any purpose. You might call it the "Universal Donor" of colors. It stands for truth and purity and as such, may be used best for cleansing and protection. This color also may be used for any type of healing. Any time that you don't know or aren't sure what color to use for a given application — you can always use WHITE without any adverse effects. Since it contains all of the colors of the spectrum, its inherent ability, like a prism, is to isolate and send the needed color to heal.

YELLOW:

This color works through the mind to enhance intellect, aspiration, and inspiration. Its energies are uplifting and cheerful. It may be helpful in creating a stronger sense of concentration.

CHAPTER 5

RITUAL

Ritual is used as an aid in healing, meditation, worship, protection, and purification of the energies. It is a tool for accomplishing one's objectives and goals.

A ritual is an established format for a ceremony. This includes any words spoken or any actions necessary for completion of the act.

Remember that all ritual is symbolic and as such is able to harness and focus energy. It may also utilize aspects of ancient occult civilizations and their mystical symbologies. What makes these symbols so powerful is simply the thought energy that has been given them, by so many, over the centuries.

For some, ritual is not necessary as their own strength of will creates the needed vibrations to effect a change or to induce an outcome. This is really nothing more than the power of positive thinking and is just as effective.

While there is no rigid format for the application of ritual, there are a few basic guidelines to follow:

1. Make sure that your motivation is proper. There is no need to incur Karmic Debt for your actions. The fact is that you shouldn't want the ritual to be effective unless it is for "the highest and best interests of all persons concerned."

2. Take responsibility for your actions. If you make an error in judgment, don't let it go on uncorrected. Remember, "what goes around, comes around," even if in a different lifetime.

3. Always begin any ritual by placing yourself in a state of protection with "The White Light" and by "Grounding Your Energies."

4. Always call upon the highest of positive energies in the Universe for assistance and guidance. These energies may be composed of the Master Teachers, your Spirit Guides and your Guardian Angels.

The most common forms of ritual involve the use of incense, candles, spiritual baths, salt, water, eggs, and their application through symbology.

CANDLES

A candle may be "dressed" or "magnetized" so as to permeate the atmosphere with a desired energy. While burning, it has the ability to intensify thoughts and desires. Once these thoughts and desires reach the ethers, they open the road for the desired outcome. Burning a candle is a way of asking the Universe for assistance. It will always respond if it is for your highest and best interest.

DRESSING A CANDLE:

One may use any type of candle. The main significance is in the color being used. It is suggested, however, that one should use a glass-encased candle. There are several types, easily purchased at the supermarket or metaphysical bookstores.

A candle should always be dressed before it is used. It is preferable that the person using the candle should prepare or dress it himself. This will increase its effectiveness. There are special types of anointing oils on the market, however, it is not necessary to use them. One may simply use a pure brand of olive oil for any purpose. Although it is not colored it will still produce the desired effect.

To dress a candle is a simple process. Anoint it with oil by rubbing it around the center. Next, rub from the center to the top using an upward stroke. Finally, rub from the center to the bottom using a downward stroke.

As this is being done, it is necessary to concentrate on the desired goal. A psalm or prayer may be said over the candle, but is not necessary. One must always do what feels comfortable. A deeply concentrated thought will do.

To put out the candle, place a candle snuffer over the top. Blowing on the flame has a tendency to create an atmosphere of abruptness and will tend to decrease the effectiveness by scattering the energy.

Refer to your color chart as an aid in selecting the proper color for the maximum result. If the color needed is unobtainable, use white. It is a Universal color and may be used for any purpose.

SPIRITUAL BATHS

Spiritual Baths cleanse the auric field from negative vibrations. They also help to open up the psychic or intuitive aspect of spirituality. They may be prepared for any purpose, as their ingredients are combined symbolically to give them their influence.

To make a Spiritual Bath one should prepare it ahead of time for the number of days to be taken. The basic formula may be divided into portions and stored in the refrigerator for freshness. When using herbs, it is best to brew them until the water begins to take on their color and scent. Never use distilled water. It has been de-ionized and therefore doesn't transfer vibration. Once the mixture has cooled it may be strained. The herbs may be discarded. This would be the point at which to add any other ingredients such as flower petals, honey, holy water, salt, etc.

There are no rigid formulas for the preparation of a spiritual bath. All that is necessary is for one to be creative with the combination of ingredients. Again, the key words here are creative symbology. Please use the reference charts for assistance in selecting ingredients.

Before you plan to bathe, set out the portion of bath mixture to be used so that it will reach room temperature. You may also add about a quart of water to it if you are planning to pour it over your body, rather than soaking with it in the tub. While either method is acceptable, it is preferable to soak in the tub with the preparation. This allows the energies to more fully permeate the auric field.

Immediately after routine bathing, without drying, use your spiritual bath. It is always more effective when one prays and asks for assistance from their spiritual guides, God and their teachers. This raises the vibration of the ritual. It's preferable to dry naturally, but use a towel if you must.

CLEANSING SPRINKLES:

It is also possible to cleanse the vibrations of the home by using various bath solutions when mopping the floor, washing the walls or by lightly sprinkling the mixture around the house.

EGGS

Eggs absorb negativity and should be used uncooked and preferably cold. This technique is most effective when the egg is prayed over while being held before it is used. It is best not to eat eggs prior to a cleansing with them as this tends to reduce their effectiveness. The body builds up an immunity to them. Eggs are used to relieve physical and emotional pain and illness. They may also be used for protection while sleeping. They are most beneficial for spiritual cleansing to remove negativity.

PROTECTION WHILE SLEEPING:

Write your name in soft lead pencil on the egg. Place it at the head of your bed. Leave it there for 7 days. If it should break, throw it out by flushing it down the toilet and start over. Break the egg after 7 days and throw it out. Then replace it with a fresh one and start again. Do this when you feel the need for protection from negative influences.

MENTAL AND EMOTIONAL CLEARING:

Energize the egg, first by holding it and praying over it. Then rub it gently over the person's head, front and back. Next, over the back of the neck and down through the spinal column. This will help to create a feeling of tranquility by dispelling negative thoughts and releasing excess nervous energy.

SPIRITUAL CLEANSING:

Eggs may be used in the corners of the house to absorb psychic negativity. Make sure to place one near any entrance that is frequently used. After 7 days collect the eggs. Break and discard them in the toilet. This should also promote a more peaceful and happy feeling in the home. Repeat this practice as often as you feel it is necessary.

PAIN AND ILLNESS:

Pray over the egg as you are holding it. Ask God (or whomever you pray to) to heal your affliction. The egg will absorb the energy of the illness or pain as you rub it directly over the affected area. The egg will only be useful in treating maladies that are the result of psychic negativity. It is also helpful to cleanse your body with an egg immediately before an appointment with the doctor. It will help to insure a proper diagnosis by clearing the energies of the body.

SETTING UP YOUR SPIRITUAL ALTAR

Select an area with a flat surface that is large enough to accommodate any statues, pictures, candles, and spiritual objects that you plan to use. Remember, this is your altar. Since you will be using candles, make sure that you have chosen an area that is safe from fire hazard. It should be magnetized with your vibration. This means that it should be in an area where it will not be disturbed by others.

INCENSE

Incense cleanses and raises vibration. It creates the proper atmosphere for performing a rite or ceremony. Different scents and colors produce different types of vibrations. While some are good for spirituality, others are best suited for love and romance or luck, etc. As they burn, the essence of their color and fragrance transfers their vibrational energies to the atmosphere. It is good to burn incense frequently, as it keeps the psychic energies clear.

INCENSE FOR ENHANCEMENT OF SPIRITUAL ENERGIES:

Benediction

Frankincense

Jerusalem

Myrrh

Sandlewood

Three Kings

All kinds of church incense

NOTE: There are several types of incense that may be used. There are self-lighting powders, sticks, cones, and some that require the use of self-lighting charcoals. Any of these are acceptable to use. It is merely a matter of preference.

INCENSE FOR ENHANCEMENT OF MUNDANE ENERGIES:

Please refer to the "Color Guide for Ritual" at the end of this chapter for the various uses of colored incense.

NUMEROLOGY FOR RITUAL

In preparing Spiritual Baths/Perfumes/Candles, etc., utilize the numerological value of the characteristics listed below, FOR EXAMPLE:

If you are trying to influence a trip to Las Vegas, you might prepare a Spiritual Bath or Candle by performing the rite over a 10-day period prior to the event. In the case of preparing a cologne or perfume, you might place 10 drops of a honey/parsley solution and 8 drops of sage into the perfume in order to have enough wisdom to leave the tables, and have the material blessings for which you went. There is no set formula, so be creative.

NUMBER ONE:

Aggressiveness, Authority, Independence, Leadership, New Beginnings, Originality.

NUMBER TWO:

Balance and Harmony, Cooperation, Partnerships of all kinds, Reuniting.

NUMBER THREE:

Fertility and Creativity, Social Interaction, Spirituality.

NUMBER FOUR:

Completion, Organization, Practicality, Stability, Work.

NUMBER FIVE:

Changeability, Communication, Decisiveness, Freedom, Speculation, Travel.

NUMBER SIX:

Counseling, Family, Healing, Love, Service, Social Relationships.

NUMBER SEVEN:

Analytical, Introspection and Solitude, Mystical Powers and Intuition.

NUMBER EIGHT:

Good Judgment, Money and Material Possessions, Power, Recognition, Responsibility.

NUMBER NINE:

Compassion, Endings, Humanitarianism, Patience, Tolerance, Universal Love.

NUMBER TEN:

A turn for the better, Fortune, Gambling, Luck.

NUMBER ELEVEN:

Energy of the "1" intensified by doubling, Higher level "2" energy, Legal Matters, Limelight, Quick Decisions.

NUMBER TWELVE:

Balanced and Centered Spirituality, Devotees, Humanitarianism, Reversal.

NUMBER THIRTEEN:

Release, Transformation, Transition, Transmutation.

COMMON INGREDIENTS FOR RITUALS

INGREDIENTS	PURPOSE
Allspice	To promote harmony and balance on a social level. Helps to balance partnerships in business and marriage.
Almonds	To create a more loving nature.
Altar Oil	Anointing oil for candle dressing. May be used in spiritual preparations by magnetizing it for a specific purpose.
Basil	Protection against negativity.
Bay Leaves	Protection against negativity.

INGREDIENTS	PURPOSE
Bible Oil	Same function as Altar Oil.
Blueing	Used in spiritual baths to promote a calm, soothing, cooling influence. Also helps to relieve pain.
Camphor	Protection against negativity.
Cedar Oil	Spiritual uplifting.
Cinnamon	Love, Money, Calming influence.
Egg Shell Powder	Protection against negativity.
Epsom Salt	Draws out negativity to purify. As a bath is excellent to release tension and anxiety.
Eucalyptus	Helps to open the brow and throat centers by clearing the sinuses.
Flowers	The petals may be used for spiritual baths. Please refer to the color chart for the proper color flower.
Garlic Skin	May be burned as incense to protect against negativity.
Hazelnuts	May be boiled in the shell to prepare a spiritual bath. Also may be carried on the body as a talisman to increase the power of the mind and to gain wisdom.

INGREDIENTS	PURPOSE
Holywater	Protection against negativity.
Honey	Sweetens influences.
Lavender Buds	To promote love and romance.
Mint	Refreshes all matters. Stimulates and soothes the mind and body.
Olive Oil	May be used as an all-purpose anointing oil for candle dressing. May also be used in spiritual preparations by magnetizing it for a specific purpose.
Parsley	Has a calming effect. Helps to influence finances for the better.
Pine Oil	Protection against negativity.
Rosemary	Protection against negativity.
Sage	Promotes having the wisdom to resolve problems. Helps to build mind power.
Salt	Draws out negativity to purify.
Walnuts	May be boiled in the shell to prepare a spiritual bath to help end a situation.

INGREDIENTS	PURPOSE
Water	All types of water may be used except distilled, de-ionized, and bottled water. Water cleanses negativity and helps to clear the mind.
Yarrow Leaves	Love and romance.

NOTE: Be creative with your "symbolic combining of ingredients." Since there is no set portion for the amount of each ingredient to be used, it is suggested that you start off by using small amounts until the desired effect is achieved. Experiment as you create, but remember, "A little bit goes a long way."

RECIPES FOR RITUAL SPIRITUAL BATHS

Always remember to clear your energies before making any preparation. This may be done by clearing your mind and cleansing your auric field. (See Chapter 1, page 2, Grounding; Chapter 4, page 20, Auras.)

NOTE: Water is the main ingredient in all spiritual baths. Holywater is water that has been blessed by a priest in the Catholic Church. You may also prepare it yourself by using the Technique given on Page 66.

RELEASE ANXIETY (PSYCHIC AND PHYSICAL)

    2 Tbsp SALT
    1/4 Cup EPSOM SALT
    3/4 Cup BAKING SODA

Combine these ingredients in a tub of warm water. Soak in this for about 15 to 20 minutes.

DISPEL NEGATIVE INFLUENCES AND VIBRATIONS

1 Cup HOLYWATER

Put this ingredient in a tub of lukewarm to cool water. Say a prayer to God to help cleanse the vibrations. Make sure to also cover your head completely with the solution at some point. It is not necessary to stay under the water for more than a couple of seconds. (See the technique for Making Holywater on Page 66.)

FINANCIAL ABUNDANCE

5 Cups DRIED PARSLEY
2 Sticks CINNAMON

Brew these ingredients in a quart of water. Let it cool, then strain and discard the herbs and spice. Divide the mixture into 8 equal portions. Place one portion in a tub of cool water and store the rest. Bathe for eight consecutive days.

WISDOM AND MENTAL CLARITY

2 Cups SAGE

Brew this herb in 2 quarts of water. Let cool and strain if necessary. Divide it into 9 equal portions. Place one portion in a tub of cool water and store the rest. This bath should be taken for nine consecutive days.

STOP QUARRELS OR RENEW A FRIENDSHIP OR PARTNERSHIP

1 Stick CINNAMON

Brew the stick in a quart of water. Let cool. Remove the stick and discard. Place this mixture in a tub of cool water. Repeat the procedure until you see desired results.

PEACE AND HARMONY/HEALING TO RELIEVE PAIN

1 BLUEING BALL

Add the ball to a tub of cool water and dissolve. Soak for about 20 minutes. (This bath is excellent for the relief of sunburn.) Blueing may be purchased from various manufacturers of occult supplies. There are also stores called "BOTANICAS" listed in the phone book. Most them seem to have this ingredient or know where to get it.

WISDOM

9 HAZELNUTS

Boil the nuts in the shells for about 1½ hours. Add water as needed. Let cool. Remove the nuts and discard them. Divide into 9 equal portions. Place one portion in a cool tub of water and store the rest. Pray for guidance and wisdom. As you are working with the head center, immerse yourself completely for a couple of seconds. Repeat the bath for 9 consecutive days.

TECHNIQUE FOR MAKING HOLYWATER

Use ONLY "tap" water. Do not use de-ionized, distilled, or any kind of bottled water. The purifying process also de-ionizes them. Put the water into a glass container that has a lid. The lid retains the energy. DO NOT USE LEAD CRYSTAL.

With the lid off, place your Positive Hand over the top and your Negative Hand over the bottom. As you do this, say a prayer to God for assistance with the blessing, or say an affirmation relating to the purpose for which the water is to be used. This magnetizes the water with the desired energy. Seal the container and keep it on your Spiritual Altar so that it remains within the highest, most spiritual energy area of your home.

When using the water, it is best to pour the amount needed into a receptacle with the other ingredients to be used for a particular bath. The receptacle should be reserved for this purpose only. Always remember to pour the water needed, rather than to reach into the container with your hand. If you touch the water without clearing your energy, it may pick up unwanted vibrations. Always keep the lid closed when not in use, so that the energized water remains at its maximum effectiveness.

An additional way of enhancing the magnetism of the Holywater is to put a small, properly cleansed and cleared, quartz crystal into the water just before you magnetize it. Leave the crystal in the container. When you have used all of the water, remove the crystal and clear its vibration for the next usage. Of course, it would be best to continue to use the same crystal, as it naturally retains some of the magnetized energy and will be more effective than changing to a different crystal each time.

COLOR GUIDE TO RITUAL

COLOR	SPIRITUAL ASPECT
BLUE	Trance Mediumship/Spiritual Devotion
GREEN	Healing Abilities
INDIGO	Intuition/Visualization/Clairaudience
PINK	Unconditional Love (Universal)
RED	Root or Life-Force of Psychic Centers
VIOLET	Mysticism/Spirituality/Transmutation
WHITE	Cleansing and Protection from Negativity. May be used for any purpose.
YELLOW	Astral Travel/Empathy

COLOR	MATERIAL ASPECT
BLUE	Peace and Harmony/Open Communication
BROWN and EARTH TONES	Grounding your energies/Neutrality/Material Possessions
GREEN	Luck/Financial Prosperity/Fertility
INDIGO	Expels negative thoughts and desires

ORANGE	Social Activity/Organization & Development
PINK	Union or Reunion in love matters/To release depression
RED	Passion/Sexual Energies (in relationships)
VIOLET	Power and Control/Imagination
WHITE	Universal Energy and may be designated for any purpose
YELLOW	Concentration/Inspiration/Mood Elevator/ Attraction and Charisma
NOTE:	For Use of Color for Healing refer to Chapter 4.

CHAPTER 6

THE ASTRAL BODY

The astral body is an exact duplicate of the physical body but is composed of a much finer matter, appearing blueish-gray in color. This matter is a form of energy moving at a certain vibratory rate, which allows it to take form as a duplicate of the body. This is the part which astrally projects and may become visable to others at times. It is always connected as if by an invisible umbilical cord or energy which allows one to return safely at will to the physical body. This vital link becomes disconnected from the physical body when death occurs. After separation from the physical body, it stays for a time on the astral plane of existence where it will develop and nourish as a spiritual body. In this new dimension it will manifest form through the vibration of color. As with the aura, each layer of color in the astral body or "shell" denotes the accompanying mental and emotional vibrational qualities of its true essence.

ASTRAL PROJECTION

Astral projection is the ability to separate the astral shell from the physical body. Once free, the astral body may travel to any of the numerous dimensions in the ethers. It is also possible to project the astral body to any location on the Earth or Spirit Realm, as well as back into the body, simply through a conscious focusing of the will.

Since our vibratory rate becomes so highly increased in this state, we have the ability to penetrate through matter. The fact is that you can actually change your physical appearance at will through thought or desire.

You are also capable of seeing even though the physical eyes may be closed. You need only think that you can see and so you are able.

Apparently, the astral body only needs spiritual nourishment. Food seems to be a "physical" necessity and really has no place during the astral journey. The senses of touch and smell seem to be relatively deadened, however, they are still functional during an out-of-body experience.

It is important to remember that journeys on the astral plane are extensions of your own consciousness. In the beginning, we start out by creating a prototype of the earth plane as we know it. Later, as we become more experienced with projection efforts, we realize that that is no longer necessary. Consequently, we begin to let the flow of the universe take over and guide us to those levels of vibration that are for our highest and best interests. Once we are able to do this, we find many different worlds to visit in time and space. It becomes apparent that there are many realities and life forms in other dimensions. By remaining open-minded about what may be experienced, we are able to learn of these dimensions while we form new conceptual beliefs about their existence.

While experimenting with the various levels or dimensions, it is vital that you keep your mind and attention focused on what you are trying to do or accomplish. It is very easy to become side-tracked with a thought, and "poof," like magic, in a moment, you are in a different environment and not quite sure where you really are. It can be rather confusing in the beginning until you learn to develop control of your thoughts, emotions, and desires. For this reason, it is suggested that you confine your journeys, in the beginning, to the immediate vicinity of your body. As you gain control and confidence, you can start to travel a bit farther.

It is important to know and believe that you can always return to your body at will. In fact, any mental, emotional, or physical trauma seems to bring one back to the body immediately. It seems to have a great deal to do with any strong desire or necessity for your physical well-being. It is a common fear that somehow you will get disconnected from your body and become unable to return. However, with practice, the fear will be eradicated. Once you are comfortable and secure with leaving and returning to the body, you may then venture into the other dimensions of the etheric realm.

You may try to astrally project as often as you like. The only concern is that one must never allow themself to become obsessed with trying to do it. Practice is good but should be done in moderation. One attempt a day should prove sufficient for development purposes.

There is no set time span in which one will accomplish their first astral projection. This strictly depends on the individual. Of course, much of this depends on how quickly one is able to learn to relax and to visualize the techniques so that they can let go of the physical.

The next question might be, "How do I know if I've projected?" Here are some possible explanations. Many people actually see themselves floating or hovering above their body. However, they usually return quickly when they realize what has occurred. They may become afraid.

This may create an emotional response which can cause them to return almost instantaneously to the body. Sometimes, the experience is too much for them to cope with, psychologically. In that case, the mind creates a block by erasing recall of the event. Fortunately, that doesn't always happen. At any rate, we will consciously remember all of these experiences when we have reached a high enough level of spiritual development; that is, when we have learned to open the brow and crown chakras. Remember, these are the areas which control the mind.

Many of us project nightly but do not realize that it is happening because it occurs during the time that we sleep and dream. In fact, usually when we dream of flying freely without physical support it is a sign of having projected. Since our mind can logically assume that the dream is not real, "it is safe" to allow us to remember the experience. While viewing the imagery of the dream state, the dreamer usually experiences a series of incongruous events. During an out-of-body experience, the environment takes on a seeming consistency, as if in the real world.

Another, not so common proof, comes through the ability of a person to perceive the bodily presence of the experimenter while in the "out-of-body" state. Likewise, the projected body is able to see and bring to consciousness, everything that has been observed while in that location. Upon return to the physical body, notes should be recorded in complete detail regarding the actions and appearance of the person or place visited. These findings may be verified for accuracy.

The development and practice of astral projection requires a great deal of dedication and self-discipline. However, once free from the physical body, one is able to grow and develop psychically and spiritually on the astral level. Of course, by working on two levels at the same time, the physical and the astral, one is able to work through Karmic situations more quickly and effectively. Remember that "Karmic" doesn't necessarily mean "debt." It also refers to the lessons needed to heighten our levels of cosmic consciousness.

It is also a way of preparing for the transition from the physical to the astral planes of existence. Through conscious astral projection, we learn to release our fears about the death experience and the existence of "the hereafter." After all, if you've been there, you know that it exists.

DEVELOPMENT TECHNIQUE FOR ASTRAL PROJECTION

Eat lightly or fast if possible before an out-of-body attempt. This will assist the vibratory rate of the body in being able to move at a higher frequency. When the body's attention is directed to the digestive processes its vibration becomes quite dense. For this reason it becomes an obstruction rather than an aid.

Have your journal ready to record all of your projection efforts. Note where in the room you decided to go, sensations experienced during the attempt and any findings that you have. Date and time your entries. Also include a brief description of any unusual experiences that might be important later.

Practice at a time and in a place where you will be completely free from distractions. Make sure that you have set aside enough time to practice so that you will not feel rushed or worried about keeping some other commitment.

Remove all metal and/or jewelry so that you cannot be distracted by it should your body roll on or press against it during the projection. Any clothing that could possibly restrict freedom of movement should be avoided as should any tight fitting clothing which could impair breathing freely. Make sure that your body will be warm enough during the out-of-body attempt. Remember, the temperature of the body drops while in an altered state of consciousness such as the "alpha" level, which one goes into as they are falling asleep. Above all, make sure that you are completely comfortable.

Darkening the room will be helpful in performing the visual techniques necessary to reach the projection state. However, the room should not be completely blacked out. A minimum of light will allow the mind's eye to see with the eyes closed.

Do not sit up during the attempt or it will probably void the conditions by bringing you back to the feeling of normal waking awareness.

Before attempting to leave the body, make sure that you understand the techniques for returning.

Set up a blue light in such a manner as to project its color directly over your entire body if possible. Otherwise, focus it over the Third Eye Center. Blue is the color of meditative activity and of spirituality. As such, it will help to relax the physical body, while at the same time, stimulating the psychic centers in preparation for the projection. While it is not necessary, it will prove beneficial as an aid to any visualization techniques.

It may be of extreme benefit to position large pieces of clear quartz crystal around your body during the attempt. This will greatly increase the vibratory rate of your energy. Lay in a comfortable position. The arms should be at the sides. The spine and neck should be straight and the legs uncrossed. The head should be facing magnetic north with the feet to the south. If you have any difficulty with this you can buy an inexpensive compass in most auto parts stores, drugstores or army surplus stores. This is a good investment as it gives more accuracy and it can be used for other metaphysical applications, one of which is setting up crystal generators.

The crystals may even be magnetized for the purpose of projection merely by focusing your thoughts while holding them in your positive hand. In this manner, the energies are stored in the gems and made ready for usage. The pointed ends should be placed facing the body. When finished with the projection attempt, put the crystals away in an insulated box.

Remember to use crystals with care since they will reinforce your thought transmissions, negative or positive. If you are having difficulty in keeping a positive attitude in your attempts, make sure to clear the gems with salt and put them away. In this particular case, they could be more of a hindrance than a help.

Ground yourself and place yourself in a complete state of protection by using the White God Light. Make sure to do this as it is a major key to always having a trouble-free return to the physical plane from the projected state.

Once you assume your position, begin breathing deeply and slowly from the diaphram. Feel every part of your body relaxing, one part at a time. To do this, place all of your concentration on each area individually. As you inhale, feel the section you are focusing on become very tense and rigid. As you exhale, feel the total sense of relaxation as your body begins to feel light and airy. Imagine that you are becoming weightless. As you breathe, notice the feel of the air as it circulates through your body. Periodically give yourself the suggestion that you will remember all that you are experiencing. Next, increase your vibration by practicing one of the visualization techniques for leaving the body.

Periodically tell yourself that your etheric or astral body is actually beginning to lift and separate from your physical body. Try to feel the sensation that the suggestion produces. Continue to stimulate the process of separation by imagining or visualizing yourself moving away from your body and then look at yourself lying there from the projected state.

Once in the separation state, you may return at any time, merely by the thought or desire to do so. However, make sure that you limit your excursions to the room in the beginning, until you get your astral bearings so that you do not become confused and frightened when trying to return. It is important to remain calm so as to maintain your thought sequence without distraction. Remember, if your thoughts wander, you could find yourself almost anywhere. So be careful. Ease into projecting. There's no need to rush.

Later, after you have more practice with travelling astrally, and are confident that you can leave and return with complete safety, then before you do your projecting exercise, you can select a place you would like to visit. It may be either on the earth plane or on the astral plane. However, it is extremely important to have absolute clarity of purpose in order to avoid misdirection of your thoughts. So decide what it is that you want to do when you get there. Again, let me make a VERY STRONG SUGGESTION. Wait to do this until you have logged some "astral hours" and just remain in your room in the beginning.

DEVELOPMENT TECHNIQUES FOR ASTRAL PROJECTION

Remember to keep your complete attention focused on what you are doing. Any distracting thoughts could inhibit the projection attempt.

(CONSCIOUS PROJECTION DURING WAKING HOURS)

1. Visualize yourself stretching outward as if to reach or touch the wall. You can imagine that you become almost rubbery as if to be elastic as you continue to reach.

2. Visualize yourself turning away from your body. Visualize it sitting or lying in position while you are moving away from it.

3. Visualize a spiral of white light or a vortex of energy surrounding your body. Next, see it spinning and whirling as it lifts you up and out of the body.

4. Focus your consciousness on an area above your body. Feel yourself merging toward it as if to become part of that space.

5. Feel yourself becoming lighter and lighter. At the same time, tell yourself how wonderful it would be to experience the sensation of floating, like a cloud. Then feel yourself start to float toward an object in the room.

6. Practice projecting your mind to another location. At first it will be easier by transferring your consciousness to a familiar setting. Allow yourself to visualize everything that is happening. The process of logic tends to distract the attention and could void the out-of-body attempt. Upon completion record your experiences.

7. Play a guided meditation tape for astral projection. They are easily attainable at metaphysical bookstores.

(PROJECTION THROUGH THE DREAM STATE)

1. Train yourself to become a "lucid dreamer." To do this, program your subconscious every night before you go to

sleep. Tell yourself over and over that not only will you remember your dreams, but that you will be completely aware that you are dreaming. It may take awhile to develop your dream skills, but be patient. Once you have mastered this part of the technique, the rest is easy.

2. The next step is to induce dreams of flying without the aid of any type of equipment. To do this requires that you program your subconscious nightly, before going to sleep. Tell yourself repeatedly that you want to fly in your dreams. Eventually, with practice, you will accomplish this part of the objective. When, in fact, you do experience a flying dream, you will be "lucid" enough to conduct an out-of-body experience by consciously willing yourself to fly through the astral or to visit some place on the earth plane. Remember to fly low enough to the ground so as to keep track of your surroundings. Also remember everything can look very different from a new height perspective. You could easily become lost or disoriented until you get accustomed to this method of travel. So go slow and low while you get your bearings. Later on you can experiment more.

3. The procedure for returning to the physical in the present moment of now is the same as for the rest of the techniques previously discussed.

(RETURNING TO THE BODY)

There are several methods in which to return to the physical body. Experiment with them and determine which is best suited to your needs.

1. You may think yourself back by seeing or imaging that you are in your body.

2. Give yourself a key thought, word, or mental image on which to focus as a signal to return to the physical.

3. Merely will yourself back into your body.

4. Mentally will some part of your body to move. The process of stirring about causes the body to bring you back to a state of normal waking consciousness.

5. See yourself going back in the direction from where you came. This will help to guide you in the proper direction. From there, visualize a "silver cord" connected to your navel. Your body will guide you the rest of the way.

6. Just keep following the cord until you return safely to your body.

CHAPTER 7

PAST LIVES / KARMA / DEJA VU

WHAT IS REINCARNATION?

Reincarnation is the conceptual belief that an individual may experience more than one lifetime. It is an extension of the concept of life after death. Not only is one able to continue life in the spiritual sense; he may also be born again physically for the purpose of spiritual growth and development of the soul. While there can be many physical lifetimes, there is only one soul, through which one is able to reestablish his link to the past. It serves as a collective consciousness and has complete memory recall of prior lives. This memory can be stimulated or recalled in a variety of ways. The most commonly accepted methods include past life regressions through hypnosis or guided meditation, the injection of truth serum into the bloodstream, and psychic readings.

There are also certain indicators of past life involvement. Sometimes one dreams of the past. Usually, however, it is expressed through one's natural tendencies and abilities in various aspects of life. The signs may also be seen in cases where one has a knowledge of the "how-tos" and "whys" of various procedures and techniques as well as a general knowledge of that field without having previously studied its particulars. This type of occurrence is very common. Another "almost sure sign" of past life involvement is when someone has a very strong interest in or aversion to something beyond the norm (which can sometimes reach phobia or obsession levels).

SOME EXAMPLES: A person might have a great love or fear of certain kinds of creatures such as dogs, snakes, spiders, etc., even if they aren't around or own such an animal. Or they might have a great fondness for a particular period in time or a particular country — even though they have never visited the country. They might decide to become an artist or musician or doctor, even though there are no role models in their family and no understandable reason for doing so. They simply KNOW that they must be that type of person and nothing can stop them. These are all examples of "carry-over" memories from past lives. Childhood genius is also usually "carry-over" such as Mozart, etc. The soul carries an indelible imprint of these memories and sometimes they seem to surface and demand to be resolved. This is Karma.

WHAT IS KARMA?

Karma is a Sanscrit word that means "ACTION which brings REACTION." The concept of Karma is the basis for one's return to the earth plane to be born again in physical embodiment. It deals with the Law of Cause and Effect. It is the principle of "What Ye Sow, So Shall Ye Reap." If you plant a watermelon seed you won't get an apple. This does not apply merely to this lifetime but can apply to any other lifetime we have ever lived. This includes good actions as well as bad. Karma does not necessarily refer to a spiritual debt or to repayment of a bad deed. It may also be for us to experience or to help someone else experience a growth lesson. In any case, Karma deals with the spiritual progression and evolution of the soul toward Cosmic Perfection and Reunion with the One Source (no matter what you call IT). A common belief is that Karmic lessons deal with only the past lives of an individual. This is only partly correct. They also deal with the present. In fact, frequently, Karmic influences that are created in one lifetime are resolved during the same incarnation. Another common belief is that the "payback" is always with the same person that the Karma is created with. This is also not entirely correct. Sometimes it is true. However, there are times when Karma is created with one person and an entirely different person is the instrument for the resolution. There is an expression, "Instant Karma," which is used in some metaphysical circles. The more evolved and progressed one becomes on the path of "Self-Realization," the quicker their Karma seems to come back to them. Sometimes it seems to "come back instantly" — that is to say, almost as soon as it is created.

WHAT IS DEJA VU?

Deja Vu is also considered to be part of the past life experience. It is the conscious realization, or impression, that one has already, at some time in the past, experienced what is happening at the present moment. While he might not understand how or why he remembers this event, he somehow knows that he has already experienced it. Some possible explanations that may help in obtaining understanding of this phenomenon are as follows:

1. It could be a product of precognition received during the dream state.

2. One may have actually gone through the same experience in a prior time, the only change being the people and place of occurrence.

3. It might be a similar experience or activity that instantaneously sparks recall of the past through the "Collective Consciousness of the Soul."

4. Another possibility has been the result of some scientific research into accelerated thought, i.e., thoughts which occur so quickly that a situation is analyzed and played out in the mind all in a split second just before it actually occurs.

WHY IS IT IMPORTANT TO KNOW ABOUT A PAST INCARNATION?

One may be able to release unnecessary illness, phobias, or fears and gain a better understanding of recurring patterns and cycles in his life. The key here is not to stop at finding out about the past, but to work to release it in the present by accepting its true origin. Frequently, we hold on to certain aspects of our life that truly have no bearing on the present. Because we are used to carrying a burden, we tend to think of it in terms of it always being with us. In essence, our thoughts confine us to a Karmic situation that is merely a carry-over from the past. By undergoing steps to identify our past lives, we can free ourselves from these ties by understanding and accepting what has happened in the past. Acceptance is one of the great responsibilities of the Karmic lesson. First we must accept, then we can let go.

CHAPTER 8

DREAM INTERPRETATION

The dream mind is a balance system for the psyche. As such, it enables one to maintain mental and emotional equilibrium. It is equivalent to a motion picture screen viewing one's innermost feelings, emotions, attitudes, and beliefs about oneself and others around him. It also captures one's belief of others' perceptions of him.

The dream mind does not employ self-deception as a defense mechanism to hide the truth. Its messages are honest and direct. If one generally sees himself as a positive, assertive and self-confident individual in real life, he will generally see himself from the same vantage point in his dreams. On the other hand, if one views himself as a passive, introverted person it is a good indication that he feels the same way about himself in reality. Whatever the personality traits, conceptual beliefs and behavioral patterns may be, one will clearly see them expressed in his dreams.

The average individual experiences 4 to 5 cycles of dream activity during the night, with each cycle lasting approximately 90 minutes. The first cycle is primarily a state of deep relaxation and sleep. Subsequent cycles are considered to be the REM (Rapid Eye Movement) stage. The eye movements indicate that one is viewing the imagery of the dream or subconscious mind.

Everyone dreams, although not everyone recalls the activity. However, in time, by consciously programming the inner mind with repeated affirmations that one will remember his dreams, progress is assured. It is best to work with programming immediately before going to sleep. Remember, it is your subconscious mind that manifests through the dream state. It is also most helpful to suggest to the subconscious mind the reason you are trying to remember your dreams.

If one forgets his dream or doesn't understand a symbol, it will manifest again and again, in a variety of ways, until it is consciously related so that it may be released. There is another type of dream which belongs with this category which is a "recurring" dream. It is exactly the same each time it occurs. It begins at the same place, progresses in the same way and ends at the same place. It is like playing a piece of movie film through your mind, always the same strip of film. This type of dream sometimes continues at intervals for several years. Sometimes a person outgrows whatever the message is about and sometimes he resolves the situation. When this happens the dream generally doesn't occur again. Any type of dream in this category is an indication that a person is "stuck" in the area that the dream pertains to.

Various stimuli may affect the physical body and could alter the dream imagery. For example, sexual dream activity could result in orgasm. A full bladder could result in dreaming of urinating and could simultaneously induce urination while sleeping. The ingestion of drugs, alcohol or any mind-altering substance can also alter the dreamstate. As we all know, these substances can affect our inhibitory factors and therefore, should not be interpreted, as they are not accurate representations of the subconscious mind. Food eaten before going to bed, such as the evening meal and/or snacks, can affect dreams and should be noted for reference.

Some people dream in color, while others dream in black and white. It seems that those who dream in color have better usage of the third eye in visualization techniques than those who dream only in black and white. Also the "color dreamers" seem to have dreams involving the other senses, i.e., smell, sound, etc., more than the "black and white dreamers."

Dreams of death usually deal with concepts of change, or transition and growth in one's life. These dreams usually represent the end of a situation or relationship in order to create the energy for a new beginning. It is good to question the literal meanings of your dreams too. Sometimes they will apply. Precognitive dreams foretell of events to come in the future. Clairvoyant dreams offer images of events that are happening during the time span of the actual dream. Some clairvoyant dreams are really forms of astral travel wherein the astral body has separated from the physical body in order to travel to various locations in the world or to other dimensions. In some cases, the events are recalled to memory upon conscious awakening.

Many psychic dreams are also called Lucid Dreams, inasmuch as the dreamer is consciously aware that he is dreaming, while he is dreaming. You will be able to experience lucid dreaming by programming or telling yourself to do so, just prior to going to sleep. Be patient — it takes time to gain control of the dream state.

PARTICIPATION IN YOUR DREAM

Were you an active participant or an observer? Observation of issues tends to indicate precognition, objectivity and a passive stand on issues. Participation tends to indicate a more aggressive or assertive nature, a doer, release through the physical body and spontaneity.

RECORDING YOUR DREAMS

1. Always keep a paper, pen and flashlight handy at your bedside for recording your notes. Call this your "Dream Journal." Always date and time your entries for future reference.

2. When you wake up, lie still for a few minutes and recap your experiences. Then record them in their fullest detail. Do this before you get out of bed, before you speak to anyone, or before you begin the day's activities. If you don't, you will most likely forget 95% of your dream. Even if you think that you can't remember very much, write it anyway. You will be surprised the first few times that you do this to see just how many details are right on the edge of your mind and are brought forth when you begin to write. It is imperative for success that you do this BEFORE you do anything else.

3. Before going to sleep, tell yourself that you will remember your dreams. Ask your "higher self" to guide you by presenting the information necessary to your highest and best interests. Write a brief recap of the day's events and any ongoing situations that could psychologically

influence your dream. For example, any situation that weighs heavily upon your mind. This will serve as a reference. Date and time this also.

INTERPRETING YOUR DREAM

Record your dream in as much detail as possible, in event sequence. Go through and underline the adjectives, nouns, and verbs. List these items without trying to relate them. Now list their meanings from the "Personal Dream Symbology" chart which you have created. Then read the symbolic interpretation in the same sequence as the underlined words. This is one major part of the interpretation. The next step is to relate these interpretations to the current activities, feelings, and thoughts in your life. How do they tie in? Record your findings.

CHAPTER 9

INTUITIVE READING
STYLES & TECHNIQUES

All forms of intuitive readings are designed to give the type of positive reinforcement and information necessary for aligning one's life circumstances with a desired outcome. For the purpose of objectivity, it is best to have a reading by someone other than oneself, or someone you know on an intimate or family basis.

It is suggested to have a reading or consultation depending upon personal necessity. The usual time frame for a forecast of general events varies from 6 months to 1 year. Depending upon one's social interaction with others and business involvements, the intervals will be more or less frequent. However, one should not feel that he must wait a designated interval if at a later date (after the initial consultation), he has questions on new or existing matters.

Consultations are intended to enlighten one's perceptions on such matters as business, health, finance, relationships, love, family matters, legal matters, and spirituality, though not limited to these subjects, of course.

Make sure that the querent (person asking questions) knows that it is all right to ask questions in order to obtain clarification on the information being given.

Readings should always be handled in a professional and confidential manner. If the client is relaxed, it will make him more receptive to your energy, thereby enabling you, the reader, to be a more open and effective channel. One point that is very important, especially when you are reading for a person who knows or is related to another of your clients, is that you assure them that their reading will be kept in strictest confidence. Many times they will say that it doesn't matter. However, simply tell them that if they wish the other person to know any of the details of their reading that it is up to them to tell the other person. You will not. This generates a feeling of trust and confidence in your professionalism. Be absolutely certain that you adhere to this precept or you can get yourself into difficult situations and possibly lose clients. One last word about this is that you must use your common sense in such matters. Should someone tell you that they are planning to take their own or someone else's life, it would be your duty to see that the proper individuals know about it. This is an extreme situation, but it could happen, as many people who are very depressed come to readers hoping to have them "solve all of their problems." Use good sense and you will be fine.

WHAT YOU CAN SAY - LEGALLY:

Legally, one is not allowed to "tell the future." This means that one must preface all statements with ambiguous phrases such as:

"maybe," "possibly," "perhaps," "might,"
"may happen," "it could happen," etc.

Legally, one is not allowed to diagnose any illness, mental or physical; nor can one prescribe any form of remedy for any condition or type of illness. By telling someone that they are ill or have an affliction, it could psychosomatically induce it to happen if it hasn't already manifested.

There is also the possibility that your perception of the situation could be inaccurate. So why take chances? The best approach is to question them about the possibility of any weakness or condition in a particular region of the body, and if no symptoms have manifested as of yet, to periodically keep tabs on that part of the body during yearly check-ups at the doctor.

WORK AREA AND DEVELOPING YOUR SKILLS:

Select an area where you may practice your reading techniques without being disturbed. It is important to create an atmosphere of concentration in order to establish the strong vibrational energies that are needed for psychic development.

Practice on a daily basis to gain familiarity with your reading techniques. Ask friends to help you practice by giving them readings and then verifying the accuracy of the information being given. In this capacity the information is controlled and remains innocuous.

At first, you may be reluctant to trust the information that you are receiving intuitively. You will adjust in time and with practice. You will also gain greater confidence once you have mastered the intuitive meanings of the Tarot Cards or whatever method of reading you have chosen to work with. Of course, it is not necessary to use any tool such as cards. The choice is yours. It is recommended, however, that you practice the psychic development exercises outlined in this manual, as it will assist you in developing your intuitive abilities.

Be sure to ground yourself and to place yourself in a state of protection before you begin any reading, even though it may be for a friend. Anyone can pick up negativity in their auric field. This negativity can be passed on to you unintentionally. So protect yourself.

If for any reason you experience difficulty in focusing on the querent, request that they direct you with their questions. This usually makes it easier to channel information.

It is preferable that you learn one form of intuitive reading at a time and become proficient at it before beginning another. If you are uncertain as to what to choose, don't worry. You will automatically gravitate to the most suitable method for you.

SYNOPSIS OF
INTUITIVE READING TECHNIQUES

The following alphabetical list will aid you in determining what method of intuitive reading you are best suited to do. Please note that some of these methods rely solely on the use of one's intuitive abilities, and as such will be the only techniques described in the following pages of this chapter. Those that will be described are marked with a double asterisk (**). The other types of reading techniques such as Astrology, Graphology, Numerology, Palmistry, Past Life Regression, Tarot, etc., also employ the intuitive abilities. However, these techniques are more scientific and require a considerable amount of time to become really proficient with them. That is why they are not covered in detail in this book. There are many fine books available on these subjects.

ASTROLOGY:

The study of planetary influences in conjunction with the date, time, and place of one's birth. A correlation is shown between the elements of the natal chart which is constructed using the birth data and one's life to ascertain information relating to past, present, and future.

AURAS:**

The interpretation of various colors and energies surrounding the body, relating to health and emotional status.

AUTOMATIC WRITING:**

The ability to channel information from one's spirit guides and teachers through automatic writing.

CRYSTAL GAZING: (Scrying)**

This method is strictly based on one's intuitive abilities. The reader allows impressions and thoughts to come to him by focusing on the crystal ball. Quartz crystal should be used, if at all possible, even though it is more expensive than other types of material.

DREAM INTERPRETATION:

The interpretation of psychic or psychological messages presented through one's dream state. (See Chapter 8.)

GRAPHOLOGY:

The analysis of a person's handwriting. This method is best used to determine personality characteristics.

I CHING:

This is based on the Oriental philosophy of life through "The Book of Changes." Coins or yarrow sticks are cast to create a hexagram. The lines in the hexagram are then translated for the reading.

NUMEROLOGY:

The study of numbers in direct relation to one's birth date as well as the numerical value of the letters in a name and how they affect one's life.

PALMISTRY:

The study of the hands. This is used to determine personality characteristics and the possibility of various outcomes in one's life. The dominant hand showing what one accomplishes and the other hand showing his potential in life.

PAST LIFE REGRESSION:

This is a method of recalling memory from past lives. It is customarily done by a hypnotist who specializes in Past Life Regression. The hypnotist monitors the regressee and guides him through various phases and experiences of the recalled life, and insures his emotional safety.

PENDULUM (Dowsing):**

This method is best used for "yes" and "no" answers to questions. A small, preferably long, pointed, object is attached to a piece of cotton string about twelve inches long and allowed to swing back and forth until it indicates an answer by moving in a clockwise or counterclockwise motion. DOWSING is generally done with "dowsing rods" which are two pieces of metal shaped like an "L" and held, one in each hand. They are most often used out of doors and for finding metals, water, minerals, etc.

PLAYING CARDS:

The use of a regular deck of playing cards to determine the future. Each card separately and in combination with the others depicts different aspects of one's life.

PSYCHOMETRY:**

Receiving and sensing impressions by holding and/or viewing an object.

RUNES:

Stones inscribed with the various letters from an ancient Scandinavian (Viking) alphabet. Each letter pertains to a specific philosophy of life. As each Rune is drawn it becomes a direct response to one's questions.

SAND SCRIBING:**

This method is strictly based on one's intuitive abilities. The reader allows thoughts and impressions to come to him by focusing on the markings that have been made in the sand by the querent.

TAROT CARDS:

The use of 78 pictured cards (56 Major Arcana and 22 Minor Arcana), each of which presents a portion of events in your life. In combination with each other they tell a story as a whole.

TEA LEAVES:

This method requires that the querent drink a cup of tea that has been prepared using loose tea leaves. There is a series of meanings and patterns used to interpret the leaves that are left in the bottom of the cup.

TRANCE MEDIUMSHIP:**

The ability to channel one's spirit teachers and guides by bringing them into the physical body of the medium. In this manner they may verbally communicate with others to share knowledge of the astral planes and to answer questions and sometimes offer advice.

DEVELOPMENT TECHNIQUE FOR SEEING AURAS

Learning to see an aura may take some time as it depends on one's ability to use the third eye. It could happen immediately or six months from now, or any time in between, so keep practicing and trying. Begin by placing a full length mirror in front of you. It should be positioned so as to have indirect light from the sun coming in behind it. Sit approximately four to five feet away from it. Now look at the area of the body just above the head and shoulders. Try to let the eyes go out of focus. The less blinking, the better, as blinking tends to refocus the vision. Do not look directly at the body, as the auric field is above and around it. If glasses are worn, they should be removed, if possible, as an aid to defocusing the eyes. This will enable you to see the prana or health aura, and possibly with practice even the colors in your auric field.

Another technique is to stare at someone for as long as possible without blinking. Then, closing your eyes, allow their image or outline to come into focus. For maximum effect, do this in a room that is relatively dark. This will help you to see the outline of their person easier. As you develop, you can practice this under any lighting condition quite effectively.

An additional visualization technique is to place someone in front of a white or black background. There should be no pattern or print behind them, as this would tend to distract the eyes from viewing the aura. Now, keeping the eyes open, look to the areas immediately above their head and shoulders. Defocus the eyesight and try not to blink. Try to see their health aura. When you have looked for as long as possible, close your eyes and try to see their image with your third eye. Just let a picture of the light, shaped in their image, come to mind. Don't expect to see colors right away. In time, they will become visible.

Remember, these techniques are working directly with the third eye, and as such will help to unfold psychic ability. However, since the third eye is probably not accustomed to being used, it could, at first produce a mild tightening sensation of the head. This is due to the expansion of the "Brow" center. Some people never experience this phenomenon, while others feel it come and go periodically. In any case, it is not harmful to the body in any way.

Practice these exercises daily for no longer than five minutes per sitting.

Once you have learned to see colors, it will be helpful to know what they represent. Refer to the Color Guide on the next page for assistance.

COLOR GUIDE TO READING THE AURA

BLACK: This is a very negative color to find in someone's aura. It can represent malice, hatred, pessimistic thinking, or ill health. It is the absence of positive energies in the mental, physical, and/or emotional bodies.

BLUE: This expresses an energy of peace and harmony, inner balance, spiritual devotion or deep religious concepts. An excess of deep blue in the aura would indicate possible moodiness or depression.

GREEN: This would tend to indicate a person with strong ability to heal others. It could also be that a healing is being received by that individual. Green signifies prosperity.

ORANGE: This would indicate a person of strong social involvement in personal or business matters.

PINK: Pink is a display of unconditional, selfless love without sexual implication.

RED: This color usually indicates an energy of love in its passion or more physical stages. Red also represents physical energy and vitality. At times it can also represent anger or hostility and possibly even high blood pressure or extreme tension and anxiety.

VIOLET: This color expresses one who has a vivid imagination or is always creating new ideas. It is also an indicator of someone's spiritual growth and development. The more violet in the aura, the higher the vibration of the individual. This is also an indicator of a disciple-type energy and may represent a teacher or one who is involved

	in a humanitarian field of work. Violet is always present in the aura of a strong healer.
WHITE:	This is symbolic of protection. White is always present in the pranic aura of a healthy individual. Generally, white is the purest of energies and represents a positive attitude or outlook on life.
YELLOW:	Yellow indicates a person of strong mental faculty. It conveys a sense of warmth and cheerfulness in the personality. Also charisma. Excessive yellow could indicate stressed personality due to overflow of mental activity.

AUTOMATIC WRITING / INSPIRATIONAL WRITING

One form of channeling information and developing the intuition is through automatic writing. By placing yourself in a receptive and meditative state of consciousness, you are able to bring through inspiring thoughts and guidance from your subconscious mind as well as from your Spirit Teachers and Guides. This may be done two ways. One may prepare a list of questions or decide upon an issue needing clarification in his life. Or he may simply allow the spiritual energies to channel whatever information that they may feel is necessary for his highest and best interests at that time.

It is best to make a special journal for recording your information. Before beginning, note the date and time and give a brief description of the current events in your life. This will make it easier to understand and relate the messages that are received.

DEVELOPMENT TECHNIQUE FOR AUTOMATIC WRITING

1. Make sure that your journal is open and ready for use before you begin to meditate. Date, time, and give a recap of current events.

2. Ground your energies and place yourself in a total state of protection by surrounding yourself with the "White Light" of the Universe. (Refer to Chapter 1.)

3. Mentally call upon the spiritual energies that will guide you for "your highest and best interests." Invite them to share their wisdom.

4. Make sure that you are sitting properly and breathing correctly. (Refer to Chapter 3.)

5. Hold your pen in hand and your journal in your lap, ready to write.

6. Clear your mind and place yourself in a deep and relaxed meditative state.

At first, the natural tendency is to watch what you are writing. As you learn to relax while channeling, it will become easier to record with your eyes closed. This is when most automatic writing begins. Eventually you will find yourself reading information that you do not recall writing and which you "do not know" on a conscious level. This is when you know that you have been truly successful. One phenomenon that occurs with some "automatic writers" is that the writing is done very quickly, without pausing to "collect the thoughts." This is another good sign that you are succeeding.

There are also times when you will be recording your own personal thoughts as they come to you. This is referred to as

Inspirational Writing. While this may not necessarily be channeling information from your guides, it can be a form of developing your intuition and psychic ability. By stilling the mind
during meditation, the creative, higher self within, can perceive
and express various insights that deal with your life and others
or even the world as a whole.

Never allow automatic writing to become an obsession,
whereby the spiritual energies record messages of their own ac-
cord. This is an area that you must control. For your own protection you should always be conscious of your actions.

It is preferable that you practice automatic writing at a specific time that you decide, such as every morning at 9 a.m., or
every evening at 10 p.m., etc., whenever you can set aside the
extra time from your regular meditation. As always, be sure that
you will not be disturbed while doing your writing.

There is another mode of writing which can be used, and
in fact, is the mode used by the noted metaphysical writer, Ruth
Montgomery. She sits at her typewriter every morning at a specific time and literally keeps an appointment with her guides.
Some people may prefer this method rather than handwriting.
You could also use a computer if you have one. This is perfectly
all right so long as you follow the guidelines given above. When
using any kind of typed or computer format you should get a
notebook and keep all of your automatic writings together in
date sequence.

As I have said many times in this book, BE PATIENT with
yourself. All of these techniques require much practice. The
most important thing when beginning any new technique is that
you act "AS IF" you already have the results. The manifestation
will follow the application.

DEVELOPMENT TECHNIQUE FOR CRYSTAL GAZING (SCRYING)

For this method a large, round, clear, quartz crystal is used as an aid to receiving symbols and impressions psychically. The crystal ball is placed upon a black velvet cloth to enhance its reflective properties. The reader then focuses his attention while gazing intently at the crystal.

In some cases, the reader asks the querent to gently place his hands on the ball, palm side down, while mentally or verbally directing his inquiries to the reader. He then removes his hands and the reader mentally consults the energies or visions being perceived in the sphere.

The reader mentally translates and relates the information being received. He asks himself questions regarding the symbology that he is receiving and tries to relate the impressions in logical sequence as outlined in the Development Technique for Psychometry, this chapter. The only difference in this style of interpretation is that the act of psychometrizing or intuiting takes place through a neutral medium, the crystal, which contains virtually none of the querent's vibrational magnetism. Even if he has touched it briefly there is very little of his actual energy in the crystal ball, certainly nothing like an object which he has owned for some time. This is why it is important to have the querent direct his mental questions to the ball. That will leave some type of vibrational influence with which to "sense."

Again, as with psychometry, record all of your impressions clearly so as to avoid misinforming the querent.

THE PENDULUM

The pendulum is a tool for bringing subconscious thoughts and impressions such as intuition to the conscious mind. This device is a way of utilizing psychic input through the answering of "yes" and "no" questions. It may also be used for Dowsing, which is the process of locating objects that are lost, as well as finding such things as water, oil, minerals, etc. A set of dowsing rods (two), can be made by straightening out 2 metal coat hangers and then forming them into an "L" shape. The pendulum frees the conscious mind of analytical tendencies by allowing the user to remain totally unbiased regarding the information being channeled. Of course, this method will not always be needed to bring through information. However, it is an excellent way of developing one's intuition.

MAKING A PENDULUM:

To make a pendulum, take a piece of string (cotton chalk-line is best), about 12 inches long. This is long enough that it will be able to swing in a circular motion as well as back and forth. At the end of the string, attach a weighted object such as a pendant, or medallion for convenience sake. DO NOT USE LEAD CRYSTAL. It is best to use an oblong, pointed object if available. It will induce a more natural motion and will encourage the pendulum to swing easily once the neural impulses from the hand begin. Quartz crystal amplifies thoughts and transfers energy. The positive end of the crystal is pointed. It is very effective used as a pendulum. To make a crystal into a pendant, a bellcap (available in jewelry stores) may be affixed to the unpointed end with permanent glue. Bellcaps have an eye through which you can insert the string and tie it on. Some metaphysical bookstores sell handmade pendulums made from various things, but the most common ones available are from quartz crystal or wood.

HOW IT WORKS:

The querent holds the pendulum over a question which has been written on a piece of paper. He mentally or verbally asks for a "yes" or "no" answer. You must be absolutely certain to ask only one question at a time. It must be phrased in such a way that in can be answered with either a yes or no. The pendulum is not able to sort out questions or to give messages in words, when used in this manner. It is possible to use the pendulum with a board which has the letters of the alphabet. The pendulum can swing to different letters and spells out words and phrases. It is very similar to a Ouija Board, except that it is done with just one person, whereas the Ouija Board requires two. When you are more experienced you can either make, or buy such a board, if you wish to experiment with it. However, in the beginning it would be best to just use the pendulum for answering "yes" or "no" questions.

HOLDING THE PENDULUM:

For best results, hold the pendulum between the thumb and first finger of the Positive Polarity Hand, to send energy. You will notice when the pendulum is most responsive by the strength of its pivoting motion. If the string is too short or too long, it will not respond with much vigor. Try the string at several different lengths, allowing time for it to respond before changing to a new length. Do this several times until you are certain which string length the pendulum responds to the strongest for you. Then tie a single knot in the string at that place so that each time you know exactly where to hold it. At this time it is not necessary to know what the movement in different directions means. That will be explained below under — "Tuning the Pendulum." The small knot will not interfere with the energy transfer from your brain to the pendulum. However, the string should not be wrapped around any of your fingers, but permitted to hang freely. It must be unobstructed and free to move at the slightest impulse. Your arm should not be resting on anything while using the pendulum. This can block the nerve responses from coming through properly. However, if you find it extremely uncomfortable to use it this way, it is possible to support the point of the elbow (NOT THE ARM), on something with some "give" such as a pillow or a soft chair arm. Don't use a hard surface such as a table. NEVER hold the pendulum hand or arm with the other hand as this creates "cross-energy" which would give a totally unreliable reading. Hold the wrist at a 90-degree angle from the arm. This allows the pendulum to hang freely.

In the beginning, the natural tendency is to feel that the arm and hand should be tense or rigid. This is a common misunderstanding. On the contrary, it is best to relax and let the energy flow. The more you relax, the less you will consciously influence the outcome of the answer. This is what allows the intuitive aspect to come into play. It is also best to keep the mind as neutral as possible when asking a question. This will assist in providing a totally unbiased response.

TUNING THE PENDULUM:

Before you can communicate with your pendulum you must both "speak the same language." You must know how it says "yes" and how it says "no." The way you do this is called "Tuning." After you have found the correct string length and tied the small knot, ask the pendulum a number of questions for which you know the answer is "yes." Allow enough time between questions for the pendulum to "settle down" so that you know which is the answer for each question. Observe which is the predominant direction it swings. Then do the same thing with "no" questions. The direction should be opposite. Do this until you are sure which direction means which answer. This might require more than one session.

ASKING QUESTIONS:

Make a list of questions. Since the pendulum can only answer "yes" and "no" questions, make sure that they are clear and concise. They should only ask one thing at a time. You may ask for information for yourself as well as for others. In the beginning, while you are getting acquainted with this method, ask about matters on which you are unbiased and have absolutely no way of knowing the answer. This will provide the proof that you need to believe in your ability to use the pendulum effectively. Remember, the pendulum is nothing more than an extension of your own intuitive faculties. As such, it will raise your level of self-confidence. However, in the beginning, until your self-confidence is firmly established, it is best to ask only questions which will not affect your, or anyone else's, life in any significant way. Accept your answers, but don't make any important decisions based upon them until you have had considerable practice and are certain of your skill at using the pendulum.

To use the pendulum for "dowsing" to detect the geographical location of a person, water, oil, minerals, etc., use a map of the desired area to be checked. To locate lost articles within a building, procure a blueprint of the foundation. Hold the pendulum over the exact area being checked and ask your question. It is also possible to walk through an area and ask the pendulum if the object in question is there.

PHRASING THE QUESTIONS:

Do not ask questions such as — "Will I move and when will it be?" This is actually two separate questions and it also asks for a response which can't be answered by "yes" or "no." You could ask it in this way:
"Will I move?"
"Will I move within the next 6 months?"
"Will I move to another state?"
"Will I move into a two-story house?, etc."

You can continue this process for as long as you wish, letting each answer lead to the next question. Remember, allow enough time between each question to let the pendulum "settle down." It doesn't have to stop, only to slow down.

Do not ask things like, "Does he love me and will he marry me?" Again, this is two separate questions. Start simply with one question such as: "Does John love me?" It is better to use names. It makes the answer more accurate. Then, depending on the answer, just ask questions, letting one lead to the next. Very often this method is more beneficial than having a list of questions already prepared. It can sometimes lead in a very different direction than we originally thought. This is the way to take maximum advantage of your higher mind. Let it guide you. The results might amaze you.

DOWSING

Dowsing, like using the pendulum, is a method for freeing the subconscious mind from the process of analyzing the answers received. As such, it too is an excellent means for psychic development. It works on the principle that any responses received to questions are controlled by electrical impulses flowing from the brain directly into the hands to bring to consciousness the desired knowledge.

Another application for which dowsing rods can be used, much more effectively than a pendulum, is locating the auric field of a person. Since the auric field, like everything else, has electrical impulses, the dowsing rods can detect where this energy field begins. All that is necessary is for the dowser to walk toward the subject holding the dowsing rods. When the auric field of the person is reached the rods respond and move. The stronger the energy of the auric field the stronger the response of the rods. You can actually ascertain just how far out the auric field extends using this method.

Dowsing rods can be used for determining "yes" and "no" answers. However, they are best suited for finding things such as large bodies of water, oil, fertile land, as well as lost or misplaced articles. Using dowsing rods, dowsers are able to locate the precise place where wells should be dug by finding the underground water. The shape of the dowsing rods allows one to move physically through an area while using them, but the pendulum doesn't function well in this way.

MAKING DOWSING RODS:

Dowsing rods can be made by obtaining two metal coat hangers. Straighten them out and then shape them into an "L," with the short end being about four or five inches long. The long end should be about twelve inches long.

HOLDING DOWSING RODS:

The short end of the "L" is placed in each hand. The grip of the fingers should feel loose and relaxed. The hands should be lightly touching at the last joint (closest to the finger nail), while tilting very slightly at an upward angle. Neither hand should be higher than the other. The hands and rods should be pointing directly at the area in front of the dowser. The wires should be parallel to the ground.

TUNING THE DOWSING RODS:

Follow instructions for "Tuning the Pendulum." However, the rods will turn towards center or towards outside depending on the answer. After you have "tuned" them, locate something that has been placed somewhere. They are now ready for use.

PSYCHOMETRY

Psychometry is the sensing of psychic information while holding or touching an object. The article becomes a focal point for determining its history of ownership as well as the past, present, and future information directly pertaining to its owner. Over a period of time, thought forms and vibrational impressions attach themselves to an object, making it possible, for the psychic, to sense the auric field of its owner. For this reason it is best to select an item for psychometry that has been thoroughly permeated with the querent's vibration. It should be an object that has been in their possession for at least six months. It is not necessary, but is preferred. Psychometry is commonly performed on jewelry, articles of clothing, photographs and all types of personal belongings. As a matter of fact, psychometry may be used in conjunction with any object, man-made or otherwise. However, if you have a choice of objects, especially when you are beginning to learn psychometry, choose something made of metal. The primary reason for this is that metals are excellent conductors of electricity. They become highly charged with the owner's vibrational energy. Of the metals, silver is the strongest conductor, but gold and copper are also good.

DEVELOPMENT TECHNIQUE FOR PSYCHOMETRY

Make sure to have writing materials available to record any impressions that you receive. Begin by placing yourself in a state of protection after grounding your energies. Take a deep breath and relax, as you would in a meditative state. Clear any thoughts or images from your mind so that you are open and receptive.

Initially, hold the object selected, for a couple of minutes, in your negative or receiving hand. Gradually begin to allow your fingers to touch the entire surface. At this point, you may place the item in the other hand as well. Move it back and forth between both hands. Let the movement flow. Notice the energy that surrounds the querent by observing the manner in which you physically handle the object. For example, do you find yourself nervously bouncing the object from hand to hand or are you calmly stroking it and touching it? Do you feel as if you are contemplating the way that you are going to touch it next?

Now close your eyes and start to sense the emotion of the article. To do this, mentally feel yourself becoming one with its vibration. Allow yourself to feel as if you are a part of it. Determine what you are feeling emotionally. For example, are you happy, sad, depressed, irritable, fulfilled, anxious about something, excited, serious, angry, joyful, etc. This will usually indicate the owner's current state of mind as well as his personality tendencies. At the same time it may also provide a clue to situations he is now undergoing.

To find out more about the nature of the owner, ask yourself if the item is "hot" or "cold." Heat could symbolize the climate of an area where the owner lives, is going to, has been, or will be. It could also represent anger or hostility. Perhaps, it deals with an aspect of the circulatory system, such as circulation or blood pressure. It could even be energy. Use your imagination. There is no exact answer. This must be determined strictly on an intuitive level. Sometimes what seems like a ridiculous impression to you will make absolute sense to the querent. "Cold" could also symbolize a condition of the climate. It could be emotional indifference. It could represent poor circulation, or anemia. A "warm" sensation could symbolize warmth of personality. It could also indicate good circulation. Next, ask yourself if the object retains the quality of heat, warmth, or cold. If it is a retainer of energy it could represent a long term or ongoing situation. For example, retaining heat for several minutes could represent that the person carries a grudge. It could also be a physical condition of long standing, etc.

Next, try to allow a picture to form in your mind's eye and listen to any thoughts that you may hear mentally, even if they are in your own voice. The ability to hear messages is referred to as "clairaudience." At times, you may even get a hunch, that is, a sensation of knowing something without knowing why you know, but you are sure of it. Just go with the flow. Analyzing it will tend to block the information from coming through. You must learn to trust yourself. Especially you must learn, when doing intuitive readings, to trust your FIRST impression. They are usually the most accurate because they aren't influenced by analysis.

In deciphering psychic imagery, there is no set pattern for determining the meaning of various impressions received. For this reason, it may be helpful to ask yourself certain questions in order to clarify the symbols received, as well as to prompt additional, new information. In time, you will notice a pattern forming in the way that you receive and interpret symbology and mental imagery. Be creative with your interpretations. In the beginning, refer to Dream Symbology.

If for any reason you experience difficulty in focusing on an individual it may be helpful to ask yourself questions about the person, pertaining to such matters as health, family matters, residence, finances, job relations, spiritual growth, travel, changes, and romantic endeavors. One by one, mentally ask if there is anything that the person should know about, and if there are any changes about to take place. This should provide some information for you to work with.

Once you reach this level of questioning, you are entering into a purely psychic or intuitive level of reading. This is the objective for development purposes. Trust your subconscious mind to bring through the correct information.

Throughout the entire psychometry and psychic reading, record any impressions that you receive. Don't worry if they don't seem to be coherent or rational thoughts and images. In fact, some of them may seem downright silly and meaningless or of little consequence. Record them nevertheless. Remember, some of the images may foretell of events to come in the future, while others pertain to the past or present. In the beginning, it may be difficult to ascertain chronological details. This too, comes with practice.

As a guideline, question the owner of the article about the accuracy of the messages related. This may be done as the information comes to mind as long as it does not seem to break your concentration. Otherwise, verify everything after you have completed recording all of your impressions. Sometimes, asking the querent to verify information can create a situation wherein they want to talk excessively. This can be a definite distraction, and, in some cases, tends to dissipate the energy of the reading.

SAND SCRIBING

All that is required for this technique is ordinary sand and a flat tray with sides. It should be about two to three inches deep, about ten inches long, and approximately six to eight inches wide. Fill the tray about 3/4 full of sand.

Allow the querent 2 or 3 minutes to manipulate the sand into any patterns, designs or shapes he desires. He can do this with his hand or fingers, or you can provide an implement such as a bamboo chop stick or something of the kind.

There are no exact intuitive meanings of sand formations, so be free and creative in your interpretation. Just go with the flow by allowing your consciousness to interpret the hills, valleys, ridges, grooves, etc., created in the sand. For all you know, they could represent the ups and downs in the querent's life. Look for straight lines. These might represent that things are going on an even keel, lack of variation, a direct path to be taken, a direct or blunt personality, conformity or possibly even someone who wants to get things done without stopping along the way. A wavy line could possibly indicate someone who is easily influenced, or sidetracked, an easygoing personality, or someone who is a follower, going for a ride. A broken line might indicate a turbulent influence in one's life, which creates a break in the normal flow of events. It could also represent indecision or the need to stop and take a new direction in life. The possibilities for interpretation in this type of symbology are numerous. Use this as an opportunity to express your creativity and originality of thought.

Of course, as always, record your information and verify its accuracy during or after the reading.

TRANCE MEDIUMSHIP AND CHANNELING

Trance Mediumship and Channeling are the abilities to communicate with Spirit Guides and Teachers, by bringing them into the Auric Field of the medium. In this manner, Spirit can verbally communicate with others in order to share knowledge on various topics such as healing, the astral plane, or even the past events of forgotten worlds such as Atlantis. One may even ask for guidance on such matters as their personal life. There is really no limit to the type of information one may receive.

The only difference between Channeling and Trancing is that during Channeling the medium is conscious of the information being received since he does not project out-of-body. He merely steps aside and allows a Guide or Teacher to occupy the same space with him at the same time. Only one spirit is able to "come in" at a time.

During Trance, the astral body is completely projected out of the body and is free to go and learn on the astral or to travel anywhere of its choosing. During the time that the physical body is occupied by Spirit the medium is totally unaware of the information being given.

PREPARATION FOR TRANCING OR CHANNELING

There are certain things that should be done on a daily basis, in preparation to raise one's vibration for Trancing or Channeling:

1. Meditate to raise your own vibration and level of spiritual awareness.

2. Light a candle, and pray for your Guides and Teachers to bring additional light that they may better and more easily match to your vibration.

3. Cleanse your auric field. This may be done either mentally or physically.

4. Mentally or verbally speak to your Guides and Teachers. Tell them of your intent and the reasons for wanting to Trance or Channel.

5. Cleanse your home surroundings, either mentally by using the "White Light," or by burning incense. Both of these methods will clear the atmosphere of negativity, while also raising the vibration.

6. Take spiritual baths for purification of your energies.

7. Keep plenty of white flowers on your spiritual altar. Dedicate them to your Spiritual Guides and Teachers.

8. Maintain a clear glass of water on your spiritual altar. It should be changed weekly. Only use cold or cool water. The water will help to ground you while also creating a stronger sense of clarity in your soul. You may also dedicate a glass of water to your Spirit Guides and Teachers. This water may be used for cleansing your aura.

9. Food grounds the energies of the body into the material plane. Therefore, it is suggested that you eat lightly, or even fast on days when you plan to Trance or Channel.

DEVELOPMENT TECHNIQUE FOR TRANCING OR CHANNELING

Select an area to work where you will be undisturbed. It should be away from loud noises and distractions. It is best to work near your spiritual altar, as that area has already been prepared for raising the vibrational level of the energies. In any case, try to establish a special place for Trancing and Channeling, as it will build the energy and make it easier to work.

In the beginning stages of development, it is best not to work alone. It is most helpful to have someone with you. A "monitor," who is familiar with mediumship can direct questions to the spirits, as well as guiding you through various situations. The monitor is also responsible for making sure that no one touches the medium during the session. Touching the medium can create an adverse effect in the energy and can produce unpleasant physical sensations for him. It can also cause the medium to "come back into the body" too quickly which can result in a severe headache, and a strong feeling of disorientation. Remember, for yourself when you are Trancing or Channeling, or if you are present at the sessions of others, DO NOT TOUCH A MEDIUM WHO IS IN A TRANCE.

Set up a colored light bulb so that it focuses on the throat chakra of the medium. The light should be blue. It deals with the throat center and will help to open spiritual communication by raising the vibration.

It will help to establish the proper vibration by lighting a white candle and burning some incense. Sit in a comfortable and relaxed position. The palms should be upward, resting gently on the lap. The spine should be erect and the feet should be placed flat against the floor. Try to keep from bending the neck, as it too, should be straight. This is to allow for the maximum flow of energies while you work. Never cross your arms or legs, as this crosses the magnetic flow of your polarity and would make it most difficult to channel or trance.

It is permissible to sit in a lotus position, as this allows for proper spinal alignment. Even though the legs are crossed, they do not block the energies. They realign and close the circuit as each leg crosses over to touch the other.

Ground your energies and place yourself in a complete state of protection by surrounding yourself with the "White Light of the Universe." (Refer to all of the techniques described in Chapter 1.) You may also use this affirmation for Protection: "I am only receptive to energies that are for my highest and best interest."

Mentally call upon your Spirit Guides and Teachers. Request only those who are there for your "highest and best interests," to come through you as a Channel or Trance Medium.

If you are taping the session, turn the recorder on at this time. If you have a friend monitoring you, it is better to have them take care of the recorder.

Now go into a deeply relaxed and peaceful state of meditation. Try to clear any thoughts from your mind. You may meditate in silence or to music.

During your meditation, remember to keep your lips moist and slightly separated and your jaw relaxed. Swallow periodically so that your throat does not become so dry that it would make speaking difficult.

It is also a good practice exercise to try to visualize your Spirit Guides and Teachers when you feel them near. Allow a picture of them to form in your mind's eye. Don't worry if you see more than one Guide. Many people have several. Just trust the images you are receiving. In time, the images will become very clear and you will be sure of what you are seeing. Become aware of any scents or colors that they may wear in their auric field. Try and remember how they make you feel, physically and emotionally, when they are near. This process will assist you in determining the intent of certain entities, as you will become familiar with their various energies.

Upon completion of the session, the medium should drink some water and should also rub his wrists together. This will help to reconnect the physical body to the etheric or astral bodies, which have either partially or completely projected out of the body during the Trance or Channeling state.

The medium should offer a prayer, thanking the energies that have participated in the session. It takes time to develop mediumship abilities. It is something that can't be forced. The key, is frequent meditation and learning to relax.

DEVELOPMENT TECHNIQUE FOR DETERMINING THE INTENT OF A SPIRIT

Mentally project a circle of "White Light" in front of you. It should be approximately the same size as the circle of light around you. When you feel the presence of an energy, ask it to step into the "White Light." It will only be able to do so if it is of a high enough positive vibration to help you in some manner.

Once it steps into the light, you may ask it to come forward into your vibration to Channel or Trance through you. If it is unable to step into the light, tell the energy that it MUST GO BACK to the astral plane and develop, and raise its vibration. Direct the entity to search out, and follow the path of the "White Light." In this manner it will reach salvation by learning and developing spiritually.

You are probably wondering how to know if it has gone into the light, if you are unable to see it happen. In this case, go by your intuition. Ask your "higher self" to clarify the spirit's purpose for being there.

Generally, you can rely on certain indicators. For instance, if you are suddenly feeling depressed and want to cry, or if parts of the body become prickly or numb, or if you experience difficulty in breathing; these are the telltale signs of a negative energy. The lightness and gentleness of the vibration experienced will help to tell you about the nature and intent of the spirit.

Certain physical symptoms begin to manifest while a spirit is fine tuning its vibration to match yours. Don't worry if you feel irritation in the throat and feel like coughing. This is quite a natural sensation experienced during the early stages of development for Trancing or Channeling, as the Throat Chakra is developing and beginning to open. Other common physical sensations include mild nausea and dizziness (usually from nervousness), a feeling of heaviness around the neck and shoulders, a light tingle or chill over various parts of the body, and slight swelling throughout the entire being. It is also common to experience a feeling of shakiness all over. However, these symptoms usually disappear after about an hour's time.

If you are still in doubt as to the intent of an energy, then under no circumstances allow it to come into your auric field. Mentally explain that you need more time to prepare and are as yet not ready to Channel or Trance. Then ask it to separate from your vibration. If it refuses to go away from your vibration there is a good reason to think that it is not an entity that is there for your best interests. In this case DEMAND that it leave at once. Again, there is no need to worry or fear. You are still protected by the "White Light," so lower astral entities CANNOT enter your auric field.

CHAPTER 10

TESTING AND DEVELOPING YOUR PSYCHIC ABILITY

MAKING YOURSELF READY FOR SENDING OR RECEIVING:

Select a time of day for practicing these exercises when you will be undisturbed. Distractions can be most disruptive to one's sensitivity and intuitive awareness.

Begin by grounding your energies and placing yourself in a state of protection. Take a few moments to relax by placing yourself in a meditative state. This will allow you to clear your mind so that you will become sensitive to the energies psychically. You may work with your eyes open or closed. However, to close them is preferable to help in avoiding distractions.

It is important to relax and not place any expectations on yourself. Anxiety tends to block the process of sending or receiving.

Always make sure that you are sitting in a comfortable position. It is preferred that you do not cross your arms and legs. However, if you are not comfortable, it will block your receptivity. Do what is best for you.

HOW TO SEND:

When practicing exercises involving the use of objects, such as cards, select a flat surface to work on. Mentally project or send a thought and/or image to the receiver's "third-eye center." Do not allow your mind to wander from its purpose. The image must be clear. Thoughts should be limited to the name, shape, size, and color of an object. A mental picture should also be created of the image being sent if possible. Too much information can tend to confuse the receiver so try to be clear and concise.

The process of telepathic sending is just as important as receiving. Through the controlled use of thoughts and images it enhances one's ability to meditate.

HOW TO RECEIVE:

Try to let your mind go completely blank. If personal thoughts come in, allow them to filter through without trying to block them. Don't give them any additional energy by thinking about them, or the fact that you didn't close them out. This is a natural part of the process in learning to discipline yourself. With practice, your mind will become a clear and open channel.

Allow yourself to feel or sense and mentally image the information being sent to you. If a thought or image comes to mind, go with it, whether it seems logical or not. Of course, you won't be right every time, but this will get you started on the right path. Just trust yourself and go with the flow. Sometimes it can be helpful to ask yourself questions about any thoughts, symbols or images that you are receiving. For instance, if you get an image of an eagle, ask yourself what an eagle represents to you. It may provide a sort of clue to be used in deciphering and translating the information.

KEEPING A JOURNAL:

It is strongly suggested that you keep a journal and record any patterns in perception. Usually the first answer that comes to mind is correct. However, this is not always the case. For example, it may be that every third or fifth and sixth answers are correct. For this reason, it is important to determine your pattern. In my own case, if given two choices, I always take the second one that comes to mind. That is my own pattern.

Always preface your journal entries with any influencing factors that may affect your scores, such as atmospheric conditions of rain, heat and cold, your health and emotional status. This will provide an indication of "peak times" for development.

To test your psychic abilities, refer to the score sheet for the number of runs per trial. Remember to record the results. This will give you a basis for periodically checking your progress.

Sometimes in the beginning it is best to complete a series of trials before checking the correctness of your responses. It is imperative to keep your mind free from distracting thoughts. This will prevent you from becoming discouraged if you make an error. However, it is often necessary to have immediate feedback so that you learn to know "how it feels psychically" when you are correct. Experiment with both systems in determining which method works best for you.

The following exercises may be performed individually or by a group:

COLOR CARDS:

Make a set of five colored cards. They can be made from colored construction paper, or for more durability, use posterboard. They should all be made in the same shape and size, so that there are no identifying marks. (When they become old and marked, replace them).

The receiver closes his eyes and shuffles the cards. He continues to keep his eyes closed. The sender, if using two people, selects a card and either holds it himself or places it in the receiver's hand while mentally projecting the name of the color as well as visualizing it. The receiver may hold the card with both hands if desired. The receiver gives the answer to the sender so that it may be recorded. Each color has its own unique vibrational qualities. It may be helpful to refer to the color charts for healing and auras, to get a feel for the type of energy in the colors being used. It is best to completely set the pile aside from the card being used.

PLAYING CARDS:

Obtain a new deck of regular playing cards. (As the cards become old and marked, replace them). The cards are shuffled by either the sender or receiver. The sender takes a card off of the top of the deck, leaving the pile completely separate from the card being used. He then visualizes its color while mentally projecting the word "red" or "black." If the sender wishes to leave his eyes open he may stare at the back side of the card as an aid to focusing his attention. If he closes his eyes, the card may be placed in his hands in order to feel the energy of the color. As a rule, Red should provide a fairly warm and stimulating sensation in the hands. Black is relatively cool and non-stimulating. Remember, however, that everyone has their own pattern of sensing. See what sensation the colors produce for you.

COINS:

Take five coins and place each one in a separate envelope. The envelopes should be of the same making. Make sure that the envelope is opaque so as not to disclose its contents. You may use a half dollar, quarter, dime, nickel, and penny. The sender mixes the envelopes as if to be shuffling cards. Next, the sender takes the first envelope off of the stack. While he holds the envelope, he mentally projects what is in it to the receiver. He forms a mental picture of the coin while thinking its name. The answer is then recorded.

E.S.P. CARDS:

This involves the use of five symbols in a twenty-five card pack. There is a star, a circle, a rectangle, a plus sign and three rows of corresponding wavy lines. (As the cards become old and marked, replace them). The cards are shuffled by the sender and then placed separately from the card in use. This method seems to eradicate the unintentional projection of other card symbols. While the sender holds the card, he mentally projects its name and visualizes its form. The answer is then recorded.

RATE SHEET FOR TEST SCORES

Number of runs per 25 trials	Chance (5 poss. choices) (# Correct)	Aptitude GOOD (# Correct)	Aptitude EXCELLENT (# Correct)
4	20	28	32
10	50	63	69
50	250	279	293
100	500	540	560

SUGGESTED METHODS: **SYMBOLS:**

    E.S.P. Cards   Star, Circle, Plus Sign,
                                        Rectangle, Wavy Lines

    Color Cards   White, Red, Blue, Yellow,
                                        Green

    Coins   1/2 Dollar, Quarter, Dime,
                                        Nickel, Penny

SCORING:

Number of runs per 25 trials	Chance (2 poss. Choices) (# Correct)	Aptitude GOOD (# Correct)	Aptitude EXCELLENT (# Correct)
3	30	35-45	46-60

SUGGESTED METHODS: **SYMBOLS:**

    Playing Cards   (Red or Black) Color of suit

MAKING A TEST RECORD:

First determine how many runs and trials you are going to complete based on the rating sheet. Set up and head each column for every possible answer that can be given. After each answer is given, place a check mark under the column designated for that response. For correct answers, circle the check mark. Use a separate line to record each response. For example, if there will be 25 trials, there will be 25 lines. There will also be additional space allotted for each subsequent run. In other words, if there are 4 runs, there will be a total of 20 columns if 5 symbols are used in the exercise. Number each run in sequence of actual occurrence.

CHAPTER 11

DAILY GUIDE TO PSYCHIC DEVELOPMENT

1. Set up a Spiritual Altar and meditation area. This should be a quiet place where you will be undisturbed. It is preferred that no one touch your altar, as you are creating an energy field unique only to your own vibration. The more your energy builds, the more focused you will become for practicing psychic development.
2. Dress in light colors as much as possible. This attracts higher spiritual vibration.
3. Diet: There are certain foods that should be avoided as much as possible. They are caffeine or stimulants, foods that are difficult to digest such as meat, nuts and fried food. Salt and sugar should be avoided as they throw off the metabolism. When the physical body is preoccupied with the assimilation and absorption of heavy foods, it is more difficult to bring through the finer intuitive and psychic energies. For this

reason, it is best to practice the development techniques on a light or empty stomach.

4. Exercise: Get plenty of physical exercise. Try to complete at least 15 minutes of some type of aerobic activity daily to promote good circulation. If the blood flows freely throughout the entire body it will decrease the potential of energy blockages and will enhance the flow of energies in the chakras.

5. Cleanse your home of negative vibrations. This should be done at least once weekly, but is good to do on a daily basis. (Refer to the section on Ritual for various methods of cleansing.)

6. Cleanse and protect yourself daily by cleansing your aura, grounding your energies and placing the white light around yourself.

7. In the morning when you wake up, record your dreams in your journal. You may review and analyze them later.

8. Meditation: Set a routine time for meditation. This should be done when you are fully awake. Begin by doing some deep breathing exercises for two or three minutes. This will get the blood and oxygen flowing through the body and prepare you for opening the energy centers through meditation.

9. Immediately after the meditation is the best time to practice development techniques. Have a notebook and pen available to do some automatic or inspirational writing or continue whatever aspect of development you are currently working with.

10. Before going to sleep, record in your dream journal a brief recap of the day's events and any particular situation that weighs heavily on your mind. Then date it.

11. At bedtime place yourself in the White Light of the Universe for protection from psychic attack while you sleep. This will

also protect your astral body should you project out for astral travel.

APPENDIX 1

NOTES

NOTES

NOTES

NOTES

NOTES

APPENDIX 2

METAPHYSICAL/PSYCHIC EXPERIENCES

METAPHYSICAL/PSYCHIC EXPERIENCES

Record any Metaphysical or Psychic experiences that you encounter:

METAPHYSICAL/PSYCHIC EXPERIENCES

Record any Metaphysical or Psychic experiences that you encounter:

METAPHYSICAL/PSYCHIC EXPERIENCES

Record any Metaphysical or Psychic experiences that you encounter:

APPENDIX 3

PSYCHIC DEVELOPMENT
JOURNAL WORKSHEETS

CHAPTER 1 — JOURNAL WORKSHEET

CLEANSING THE ENERGY
OF THE CHAKRAS

Create your own Development Techniques
for Cleansing your Chakra Energies:

CHAPTER 1 — JOURNAL WORKSHEET

GROUNDING

Create your own Development Techniques
for Grounding your Energies:

CHAPTER 1 — JOURNAL WORKSHEET

PSYCHIC PROTECTION

Create your own Development Techniques
for Psychic Protection:

THE AURA

Create your own Development Techniques
  for Seeing Auras:

CHAPTER 3 — JOURNAL WORKSHEET

MEDITATION

Create your own Meditations:

AFFIRMATIONS

Create your own Affirmations:

CHAPTER 3 — JOURNAL WORKSHEET

GOALS AND OBJECTIVES

List your Goals and Objectives for Visualization:

CHAPTER 4 — JOURNAL WORKSHEET

METAPHYSICAL HEALING

Create your own Healing Techniques:

CHAPTER 4 — JOURNAL WORKSHEET

METAPHYSICAL HEALING RECORD

Date: Time:

Patient's Name:

Method of Treatment:

Reason for Treatment:

Results:

Date: Time:

Patient's Name:

Method of Treatment:

Reason for Treatment:

Results:

Date: Time:

Patient's Name:

Method of Treatment:

Reason for Treatment:

Results:

METAPHYSICAL HEALING
with GEMSTONES

Using the pendulum, determine which gemstones will work in affinity with your vibration for healing:

Agate — Carnelian
  — Fire
Amber
Azurite
Beryl — Aquamarine
  — Emerald
  — Golden
Chalcedony
Chrysocolla
Coral
Diamond
Fluorite
Garnet
Ivory
Jade
Jasper — Bloodstone
  — Brown
  — Green
  — Picture
  — Poppy
  — Red
  — Yellow
Lapis Lazuli
Magnetite
Malachite
Moonstone
Obsidian
Onyx
Opal

Pearl
Peridot
Pyrite
Quartz Crystal — Amethyst
  — Blue
  — Citrine
  — Clear
  — Rose
  — Rutilated
  — Smoky
  — Tourmalinated
Rhondonite
Ruby
Sapphire
Sodalite
Tiger's-Eye
Topaz
Tourmaline — Blue
  — Black
  — Cat's-Eye
  — Clear
  — Green
  — Opalized
  — Red
  — Rubellite
  — Watermelon
Turquoise
Other
Other
Other
Other
Other

CHAPTER 5 — JOURNAL WORKSHEET

RITUAL

Create your own Rituals and Spiritual Preparations:

CHAPTER 6 — JOURNAL WORKSHEET

ASTRAL PROJECTION

Create your own Visualizations and Development Techniques to induce an Out-of-Body experience:

CHAPTER 6 — JOURNAL WORKSHEET

ASTRAL PROJECTION EXPERIENCES

Date: Time:
Influencing Factors:

Method Used:
Physical Sensations Experienced:
Results:

Date: Time:
Influencing Factors:

Method Used:
Physical Sensations Experienced:
Results:

Date: Time:
Influencing Factors:

Method Used:
Physical Sensations Experienced:
Results:

PAST LIVES/KARMA

Record any aspects of your current life that you feel may be related to a Past Life experience or that you wish to explore as a possible Karmic tie. Include such things as patterns in romantic involvements, business, legal situations, accidents, family matters, personal relationships, material possessions, health, as well as innate abilities or special talents etc.:

CHAPTER 7 — JOURNAL WORKSHEET

PAST LIFE RECALL

Date: Time:
Influencing Factors:

Method:
Purpose:
Record the Information:

Date: Time:
Influencing Factors:

Method:
Purpose:
Record the Information:

Date: Time:
Influencing Factors:

Method:
Purpose:
Record the Information:

CHAPTER 7 — JOURNAL WORKSHEET

DEJA VU

Record any Deja Vu that you experience:

Date: Time:

Record the event:

Date: Time:

Record the event:

Date: Time:

Record the event:

Date: Time:

Record the event:

DREAM INTERPRETATION
PSYCHOLOGICAL INFLUENCES

There are a few basic psychological influences to consider before trying to interpret your dream. The following list of circumstances (listed alphabetically) are the most commonly found, heavily influencing factors expressed in dreams:

FAMILY INFLUENCES:

What type of family influences affect you at this time?

GOALS:

Do you have any goals in life? If so, what are they? Are they realistic? What is their time-frame?

HEALTH:

How is your health? How is the health of those persons close to you?

JOB/FINANCES:

How is your financial status at this time? Do you enjoy your work? Are you getting ready to make any changes in your career?

MATE OR LOVER:

Are you in a relationship at this time? If not, do you wish to be? If you are in a relationship, is there any stress involved? Do you feel that you are getting along with each other in a satisfactory way? If not, why?

MOOD:

What is your mental and emotional status?

RESIDENCE:

Are you comfortable in your home environment? Are you getting ready to make a change, such as moving, remodeling, taking a roommate (or spouse), removing a roommate (or spouse)?

TRANSPORTATION:

Do you have your own transportation? If so, is your vehicle in good working condition? Is it the kind of vehicle that you really want?

CHAPTER 8 — JOURNAL WORKSHEET

PERSONAL DREAM SYMBOLOGY

Before beginning to interpret any of your dreams, it is important that you create a "PERSONAL DREAM DICTIONARY." Write your own definitions to *ALL* of the symbols, objects, and situations that manifest in your dreams by determining what they represent to you, as well as how you feel about them. Remember, this is your PERSONAL dictionary. Don't ask other people what they think any of the words mean. The worst thing you can do is to look up the meanings in "dream dictionaries." It is especially important, in the beginning, that you not use these "canned definitions" taken from various books. This is absolutely essential so that you do not program yourself with some other person's meanings. One's background, environment, and experiences have a great deal to do with how one interprets various symbols and objects.

FOR EXAMPLE: Take the subject of snakes. One person might have had snakes for pets as a child, or as an adult, and feel very good about snakes. Therefore, if they dream about them, they probably wouldn't have any adverse feelings. On the other hand, another person might have been frightened by an encounter with a snake, or might even know of someone who was bitten by a snake. This person most likely would not react well to dreaming about snakes. Use this example, and apply it to many other things. You can see how important it is to create your own definitions.

I have included blank pages for you to create your Personal Dream Dictionary. For your own growth, make it as expansive as possible.

CHAPTER 8 — JOURNAL WORKSHEET

DREAM INTERPRETATION
PERSONAL DREAM SYMBOLOGY

CHAPTER 8 — JOURNAL WORKSHEET

DREAM INTERPRETATION
PERSONAL DREAM SYMBOLOGY

CHAPTER 8 — JOURNAL WORKSHEET

DREAM INTERPRETATION
PERSONAL DREAM SYMBOLOGY

CHAPTER 8 — JOURNAL WORKSHEET

DREAM INTERPRETATION
PERSONAL DREAM SYMBOLOGY

CHAPTER 8 — JOURNAL WORKSHEET

DREAM INTERPRETATION
RECORDING and INTERPRETING YOUR DREAMS

STEP 1

(Complete this section before going to sleep)

Date: Time:

Write a Brief Recap of the Day's Events:

Write a Brief Recap of Ongoing Situations:

List any Influencing Factors:

STEP 2

(Complete this section upon awakening before getting out of bed)

Record your Dream/s in Event Sequence.
Then Underline the Descriptive Adjectives, Nouns, and Verbs.

STEP 3

Transfer the Items that have been Underlined in Step 2 to this section, *in dream sequence*. Opposite each item record its interpretation from your "PERSONAL DREAM SYMBOLOGY" List.

Descriptive Adjectives, Nouns, Verbs:

Personal Symbolic Interpretation:

STEP 4

List the Psychological Influences . Then record the interpretation of each item from your "PERSONAL DREAM SYMBOLOGY" List.

Psychological Influences:

Interpretation:

STEP 5

Evaluate your Dreams:

Recap sections 3 & 4. *Record only the symbolic interpretations* of each item listed, again in *dream sequence*. Then read the information line by line. View its contents objectively, without making any further reference to the actual dream. Relate each statement to the next. Decide how your information relates to the items in Step 1.

From Step 3 — Adjectives, Nouns, Verbs (Underlined Items):

From Step 4 — Psychological Influences:

STEP 6

Final Evaluation:

How does all of this tie-in to the information given in Step 1? Record your findings.

CHAPTER 8 — JOURNAL WORKSHEET

DREAM INTERPRETATION
DREAM ANALYSIS

DREAM INTERPRETATION
DREAM ANALYSIS

CHAPTER 8 — JOURNAL WORKSHEET

DREAM INTERPRETATION
DREAM ANALYSIS

DREAM INTERPRETATION
DREAM ANALYSIS

INTUITIVE READING STYLES and TECHNIQUES
SEEING AURAS

Date: Time:

Reading For:

Influencing Factors:

Interpret the Health Aura:

Interpret the Auric Colors:

Date: Time:

Reading For:

Influencing Factors:

Interpret the Health Aura:

Interpret the Auric Colors:

Date: Time:

Reading For:

Influencing Factors:

Interpret the Health Aura:

Interpret the Auric Colors:

CHAPTER 9 — JOURNAL WORKSHEET

INTUITIVE READING STYLES and TECHNIQUES
AUTOMATIC WRITING

Date: Time:

Influencing Factors:

Physical Sensations Experienced:

Record the Information:

Date: Time:

Influencing Factors:

Physical Sensations Experienced:

Record the Information:

INTUITIVE READING STYLES and TECHNIQUES
CRYSTAL GAZING

Date: Time:

Reading For:

Influencing Factors:

Record the Information:

Date: Time:

Reading For:

Influencing Factors:

Record the Information:

CHAPTER 9 — JOURNAL WORKSHEET

INTUITIVE READING STYLES and
TECHNIQUES
CHANNELING

Date: Time:

Influencing Factors:

Physical Sensations Experienced:

Record the Information:

Date: Time:

Influencing Factors:

Physical Sensations Experienced:

Record the Information:

Date: Time:

Influencing Factors:

Physical Sensations Experienced:

Record the Information:

INTUITIVE READING STYLES and TECHNIQUES
DOWSING

Date: Time:

Questions For:

Influencing Factors:

Questions: Responses:

Date: Time:

Questions For:

Influencing Factors:

Questions: Responses:

CHAPTER 9 — JOURNAL WORKSHEET

INTUITIVE READING STYLES and TECHNIQUES
INSPIRITIONAL WRITING

Date: Time:

Influencing Factors:

Physical Sensations Experienced:

Record the Information:

Date: Time:

Influencing Factors:

Physical Sensations Experienced:

Record the Information:

INTUITIVE READING STYLES and TECHNIQUES
USING the PENDULUM

Date: Time:

Questions For:

Influencing Factors:

Questions: Responses:

Date: Time:

Questions For:

Influencing Factors:

Questions: Responses:

CHAPTER 9 — JOURNAL WORKSHEET

INTUITIVE READING STYLES and TECHNIQUES
PSYCHOMETRY

Date: Time:

Reading For:

Influencing Factors:

Record the Information:

Date: Time:

Reading For:

Influencing Factors:

Record the Information:

INTUITIVE READING STYLES and TECHNIQUES
SAND SCRIBING

Date: Time:

Reading For:

Influencing Factors:

Record the Information:

Date: Time:

Reading For:

Influencing Factors:

Record the Information:

Date: Time:

Reading For:

Influencing Factors:

Record the Information:

CHAPTER 9 — JOURNAL WORKSHEET

INTUITIVE READING STYLES and
TECHNIQUES
TRANCE MEDIUMSHIP

Date: Time:

Influencing Factors:

Physical Sensations Experienced:

Record the Information:

Date: Time:

Influencing Factors:

Physical Sensations Experienced:

Record the Information:

Date: Time:

Influencing Factors:

Physical Sensations Experienced:

Record the Information:

CHAPTER 10 — JOURNAL WORKSHEET

TESTING and DEVELOPING YOUR PSYCHIC ABILITY

Create your own Methods for Testing Psychic Ability:

CHAPTER 10 — JOURNAL WORKSHEET

TESTING and DEVELOPING YOUR PSYCHIC ABILITY
TEST RECORD

Chart your Test Runs:

CHAPTER 10 — JOURNAL WORKSHEET

TESTING and DEVELOPING YOUR
PSYCHIC ABILITY
TEST RECORD

Chart your Test Runs:

TESTING and DEVELOPING YOUR
PSYCHIC ABILITY
SCORE SHEET

Date: Time:

Influencing Factors:

Method Used:

No. of Runs: No. of Trials:

No. Possible   No. Actual

Correct Answers: Correct Answers:

Aptitude According to Rate Sheet:

Date: Time:

Influencing Factors:

Method Used:

No. of Runs: No. of Trials

No. Possible   No. Actual

Correct Answers: Correct Answers:

Aptitude According to Rate Sheet:

CHAPTER 10 — JOURNAL WORKSHEET

TESTING and DEVELOPING YOUR
PSYCHIC ABILITY
SCORE SHEET

Date: Time:

Influencing Factors:

Method Used:

No. of runs: No. of Trials:

No. Possible   No. Actual

Correct Answers: Correct Answers:

Aptitude According to Rate Sheet:

Date: Time:

Influencing Factors:

Method Used:

No. of Runs: No. of Trials:

No. Possible   No. Actual

Correct Answers: Correct Answers:

Aptitude According to Rate Sheet:

SUGGESTED READING MATERIAL

MEDITATION
Meditation   Mouni Sadhu

THE ASTRAL BODY/PSYCHIC ENERGY CENTERS
The Etheric Double   A.E. Powell
The Chakras   C.W. Leadbeater

**GENERAL INFORMATION/PARAPSYCHOLOGY
AND METAPHYSICS**
Your Psychic Powers and   Hereward Carrington
   How To Develop Them
Develop Your Psychic Skills   Enid Hoffman

AFFIRMATIONS AND POSITIVE THINKING
Creative Visualization   Shakti Gawain
Psycho-Cybernetics   Maxwell Maltz

AURAS AND THE MEANING OF COLOR
The Power of The Rays   S.G.J. Ouseley
The Human Aura   Swami Panchadasi

RITUAL/CANDLES/INCENSE/OILS/AND SPIRITUAL CLEANSING
Spiritual Cleansing   Draja Mickaharic

GEMSTONES FOR HEALING
Healing Stoned   Julia Lorusso
                                              & Joel Glick
The Crystal Book   Dael (Dale Walker)
The Spiritual Value of Gemstones   Wally Richardson
                                              & Lenora Huett

METAPHYSICAL HEALING
Magnetic Therapy   Abbot George Burke
Your Healing Hands   Richard Gordon
The Miracle of Metaphysical Healing   Evelyn M. Monahan

ASTRAL PROJECTION
Leaving The Body   D. Scott Rogo
Mental and Astral Projection   Robert E. Moser
Journeys Out Of The Body   Robert A. Monroe

DEVELOPING PSYCHIC ABILITIES

GLOSSARY

Words capitalized within brackets, are themselves defined in the Glossary. Look there for further definition.

For example: <TALISMAN>

Words for which no definition is given, but refer to a different word in the Glossary, are given in parentheses.

For example: (See Anointing Oil)

You will find many words listed in this glossary that you are familiar with. However, these definitions are given in their "metaphysical/psychic" connotations. Look them up to be sure that you understand their psychic meaning & application.

ABSENTEE HEALING: A healing that is performed without the patient being physically in the presence of the <HEALER>.

AFFIRMATION: To make a statement about something in a positive manner.

ALIGNMENT: To create "balance and harmony" within the flow of one's energies, mentally, physically, and emotionally.

ALLSPICE: A spice used in <RITUAL⟩ as an ingredient in various preparations to induce "harmony and balance" in all types of relationships. May be brewed in liquid mixtures or added dry.

ALMONDS: Used in <RITUAL> as an ingredient in various preparations to induce "a more loving nature." May be boiled in the shell, whole for liquid mixtures or used ground up. May also be carried on the person as a <TALISMAN>.

ALPHA-STATE: A state of consciousness between the active mode and the sleep state. Most psychic impressions are received while in this state of consciousness. It occurs naturally when going to sleep or waking up.

ALTAR OIL: Used primarily as an ingredient in <SPIRITUAL BATH> preparations and <CANDLE DRESSING>. (See Anointing Oil.)

ALTERED STATE: A state of consciousness which is intentionally induced, using such methods as hypnosis, visualization, meditation, drugs, etc. (Drugs have been used but are not recommended as they can deplete one's psychic abilities and pranic energies.) It is usually for the purpose of self-development.

AMPLIFIER: Something that magnifies energy.

ANOINTING OIL: A scented or plain oil used in Ritualistic practices to permeate the atmosphere with a certain energy as a way of promoting a desired outcome or circumstance.

ASTRAL BODY: (See Etheric Body.)

ASTRAL PLANES: (See Ethers.)

ASTRAL PROJECTION: The ability to lift and separate the <ETHERIC BODY> from the physical body.

ASTRAL SHELL: (See Etheric Body.)

ASTROLOGY: The study of planetary influences in conjunction with one's birth date, time, and place. A correlation is shown between the elements of the planets and one's life to ascertain information relating to the past, present & future.

ATLANTIS: Often referred to as "The Lost Continent." By legend, its existence is reputed to be ten thousand years in the past. This civilization was said to have highly evolved technology. Atlantis supposedly sank into the Atlantic Ocean. Some believe that they destroyed their own civilization as a result of misuse of their highly developed powers.

AURA: The psychic energy field surrounding the body that manifests its vibration in the form of color, reflecting one's mental, emotional and physical state of being. Its emanations are measurable and become visible through the use of <KIRLIAN PHOTOGRAPHY>.

AURA CLEANSING: The act of removing any psychic impurities from the <AURIC FIELD> of a being or object.

AURA READING: The interpretation of various colors and energies surrounding the body, relating to one's health and emotional status.

AURIC FIELD: The energy field which surrounds the body of all living entities. (See Aura.)

AUTOMATIC WRITING: The ability to <CHANNEL> one's <SPIRIT GUIDES AND TEACHERS> through writing while those entities control the movement of the hand to direct the information as they wish it to appear.

BALANCING: To properly align oneself with <COSMIC> energies of the <UNIVERSE> to restore or maintain harmony within the mental, emotional and physical bodies.

BASIL LEAVES: An herb used in <RITUAL> as an ingredient in preparations to induce "protection from negativity." May be brewed in liquid mixtures or added dry.

BAY LEAVES: An herb used in <RITUAL> as an ingredient in preparations to induce "protection from negativity." May be brewed in liquid mixtures or added dry.

BIBLE OIL: Used primarily in <SPIRITUAL BATH> preparations and <CANDLE-DRESSING>. (See Anointing Oil.)

BLOCKING: That which impedes the energies from flowing freely. It may pertain to the emotions or the physical magnetic <ALIGNMENT> of the body's energies.

BLUEING: A deep blue powdered substance made into a ball, which, when placed in a water solution, becomes a blue-colored liquid. The color is responsible for inducing a "calm, soothing, and cooling influence."

BODY-ENTERINGS: Referring to <PSYCHIC SURGERY>, whereby the psychic healers are able to operate on the human body using only their bare hands as surgical instruments. In this manner they penetrate deeply below the surface of the skin, and visibly remove diseased or damaged tissue.

CAMPHOR: A substance used in <RITUAL> as an ingredient to "repel negativity." It is placed in water to activate its properties. It is commonly found in pharmacies.

CANDLE-DRESSING: <MAGNETIZING> or energizing a candle for a specific purpose, by anointing it with oil.

CEDAR OIL: Used in <RITUAL> as an ingredient in various preparations to induce "spiritual uplifting." (See Annointing Oil.)

CENTERING: (See Balancing.)

CEREMONIAL: (See Ritual.)

CHAKRA: A psychic energy center, of which there are seven, located within the <ETHERIC BODY>. The energy centers are called by the Sanskrit word "chakra" which means "wheel" because they are believed to resemble that shape. Each center correlates to various aspects of either the physical, mental, or emotional bodies of man.

CHAKRA-BALANCING: The realignment of the magnetic energy field within a particular <CHAKRA>.

CHANNELING: Directing or focusing energy for a specific purpose. Also refers to one's ability to communicate with <SPIRIT GUIDES AND TEACHERS>, during which time the medium is conscious and aware of the information being received.

CINNAMON: A spice used as an ingredient in <RITUAL> to induce "love, money, or a calming influence." May be brewed in a liquid mixture or ground up and used dry.

CLAIRAUDIENT: One who has the ability to hear psychic transmissions of thought.

CLAIRVOYANT: One who has intuitive perception or knowledge of a situation as it actually occurs, even when not present.

CLAIRVOYANT DREAM: To dream about something while it is happening. One of the most common occurrences is dreaming of someone dying at the exact time when they die.

CLEANSING: The act of removing any physical, mental, emotional or psychic impurities in the energy of a person or thing.

CLEARING: Without changing the initial energies of an object or person, to remove any unwanted vibrations.

COINS: A method of testing one's intuitive abilities by having the subject try to visualize which coin is being presented (in a sealed envelope) while his eyes are closed.

COLLECTIVE CONSCIOUSNESS OF THE SOUL: Memory and recall of past life experiences that is stored in the soul and is realized on a subconscious or conscious level.

COLOR BREATHING: A technique for strengthening the <AURIC FIELD> through the <VISUALIZATION> of each breath as a ray of colored light coming in and circulating through the body.

COLOR CARDS: A method of testing one's intuitive abilities by having the subject try to visualize which color is being presented while his eyes are closed.

COMPLETING THE POLARITY OF A CIRCUIT: Positioning the body in such a way as to allow its energy to flow from negative to positive without any break in the flow of the current.

CONCENTRATION: The focusing of one's attention to a matter, with the exclusion of all distraction.

CONSCIOUSNESS: A state of being dealing with one's physical alertness and psychic awareness.

CONTEMPLATION: To deeply ponder or think about something.

COSMIC: (See Universe.)

COSMOS: (See Universe.)

COWRIE SHELLS: A divination process combining the use of numerology and proverbs. The shells are cast by the reader for the <QUERENT> in order to determine the numerals upon which the <READING> is based.

CREATING A CIRCUIT: A technique used in <MAGNETIC THERAPY> for creating a flow or current of energy.

CROSS-ENERGY: A condition caused by touching one hand (or arm) with the other hand, especially during a healing or using the pendulum. It creates a "psychic energy short-circuit."

CRYSTAL BALL: A spherically-shaped object made of quartz or lead crystal which is used for <CRYSTAL GAZING>.

CRYSTAL GAZING: This reading method is strictly based on one's intuitive abilities. The reader allows impressions and thoughts to come to him by focusing on the crystal ball.

CURRENT: (See Energy Current.)

DEATH: Transition, change, or the end of a situation as viewed from a metaphysical perspective.

DEJA VU: The conscious realization that one has already, at some time in the past, experienced a similar or same type of situation as that which is happening at the present time.

DISTILLED WATER: Water that has been deionized. Since there are no negative ions, it is impossible to energize or magnetically charge this type of water. Bottled drinking water is also deionized in the purification process.

DIVINATION: Any system of predicting or foretelling the future.

DIVINE: Often used in reference to God or the Supreme Power of the <UNIVERSE>. Also pertaining to that of a highly evolved spiritual nature. (See Divination.)

DIVINE PLAN: Fate or the destiny of one's life as ascribed by the higher powers of the <UNIVERSE> for one's highest and best interests.

DOMINANT EYE: The eye used when looking at something with one eye only, such as aiming a gun or bow. Usually the same side as the <DOMINANT HAND>. For those wearing glasses, it is not necessarily the eye with the best or strongest vision.

DOMINANT HAND: (See Positive Hand.)

DOWSING: A method used to receive answers to questions as well as a means of locating things through the use of two metal rods, which move together in a certain manner when indicating a response.

DOWSING RODS: Instruments used for <DOWSING>. Two separate metal rods, each of which forms the shape of an "L."

DRAWING OUT ENERGY: To withdraw or take out energy from someone or something. This may be done manually, as in <MAGNETIC THERAPY>, or mentally through thought projection.

DREAMS: Imagery of the mind during the <REM STATE> of sleep.

DREAM INTERPRETATION: Interpretation of the symbolic imagery perceived in the dream state on a psychic/psychological level.

EGG SHELL POWDER: A fine white powder made from eggshells. It is used as an ingredient in <RITUAL> to "cleanse an energy and to create an atmosphere of protection." As it is used for cleansing, only white eggs should be used. It may be used dry as a sprinkling mixture or in a liquid preparation.

ELECTRO-MAGNETIC: Electro — referring to the electrical flow of energy within the body; Magnetic — referring to the attraction of the energies which create an <ENERGY CURRENT>.

ENERGY-BALANCING: (See Polarity Balancing.)

ENERGY CENTERS: (See Chakras.)

ENERGY CURRENT: A flow of electrical impulses where the energy moves from the negative pole into the positive pole to create a current of energy.

ENERGY VORTEX: Etheric substance which takes shape in a circular motion (like a whirlpool) as if to create a spiral of energy with a vacuum effect of drawing something inside of it.

ENERGY-CHARGED WATER: Water that has been <MAGNETIZED> so as to place a desired energy into it.

EPSOM SALT: An ingredient used in <RITUAL> as an "agent to draw out negativity or to purify something." As a warm bath, it is excellent for "relief from tension and anxiety."

E.S.P.: Extra Sensory Perception. (See Psychic.)

E.S.P. CARDS: A method of testing one's intuitive abilities by having the subject try to visualize or determine by psychic means, which image, of five possible choices, is on the card that is presented to him. This is done with the eyes closed.

ETHERS: The psychic or non-physical atmosphere of other vibrational or dimensional planes of existence.

ETHERIC BODY: Often referred to as the <ASTRAL BODY> or shell. It is a duplicate of the physical body but is composed of much finer matter. This is the part of one's being which is able to lift out and separate from the physical body during <ASTRAL PROJECTION>.

ETHERIC DOUBLE: (See Etheric Body.)

EUCALYPTUS: An herb used in <RITUAL> to induce "opening of the Brow and Throat Centers." It works by opening the sinuses. Its general use is as an inhalant but it is also used in other preparations. It may be brewed in a liquid mixture or ground up and used dry.

FLOWERS: The petals of the flowers may be used in <RITUAL> as an ingredient to create a certain vibratory effect to induce a desired energy. The petals only are used and the rest is discarded. The color of the petals is the influencing factor which creates the vibrational field. They may be used fresh in liquid mixtures or may be dried and crushed and used as an incense or additive to any spiritual preparation.

FORECASTING: The process of predicting the future outcome of events via scientific or intuitive means.

GARLIC SKIN: An ingredient used in <RITUAL> to induce "protection against negativity." May be dried and ground up for use as incense or may be left on the entire cluster of garlic cloves and hung in a location where there are a lot of people passing through, such as an entrance to a house.

GEMSTONE THERAPY: The use of various gemstones, each having its own respective attributes, for the purpose of creating a desired energy field or effect upon the environment.

GENERATOR: Any source of power strong enough to magnetically charge or polarize another object with its own energy.

GRAPHOLOGY: Handwriting analysis.

GROUND: To stabilize or balance the physical, mental, or emotional energies of a person, place, or thing.

GROUNDING YOUR ENERGY: The technique used for <CENTERING> and <BALANCING> one's mental, physical and emotional energies. It is a way of connecting the cosmic energies of the <UNIVERSE> to the material energies of the earth plane, through one's person, as if to become a <GROUND> or stabilizer.

189

GUARDIAN ANGEL: A highly evolved soul in etheric form, sent by God to guide and protect one during their lifetime on the earth plane.

GUIDED CONTEMPLATION: The act of being verbally guided by someone through a <VISUALIZATION> of a subject that is being deeply pondered, during which time a visualization of the subject matter is experienced by the one in contemplation.

HAZELNUTS: Used in <RITUAL> as an ingredient in various preparations to "increase the power of the mind, concentration, and wisdom." May be boiled whole, in the shell, or ground up. May also be carried on the person as a <TALISMAN>.

HEALER: The individual performing the healing.

HEALTH AURA: The psychic energy field surrounding the physical body, which, through its appearance, displays indicators of one's physical health status.

HEREAFTER: Other etheric planes or spiritual dimensions in time and space, whereupon life, in other forms, continues to exist after physical death occurs.

HOLISTIC HEALTH: The practice of preventive medicine as well as curative methods for illnesses involving the use of natural remedies as well as metaphysical healing techniques.

HOLYWATER: An ingredient used in <RITUAL> to induce "protection against negativity." It is used as an additive to liquid mixtures for various preparations. It is tap-water which has been blessed by a religious person or yourself.

HONEY: An ingredient used in <RITUAL> to induce a "sweetening or soothing effect." Raw or processed honey may be used, but raw is preferable.

HYPNOSIS: A form of mesmerism whereby the subject is put into an <ALTERED STATE> of consciousness, and becomes extremely susceptible to suggestions given by the hypnotist.

I CHING: A type of <READING> or <FORECAST> of events based on an Oriental philosophy of life. <COINS> or <YARROW STICKS> are cast to create a hexagram. The lines in the hexagram are then broken down into two trigrams which are translated for the reading through "The Book of Changes."

IMAGERY: The pictures and images seen during a <VISUALIZATION>.

IMAGING: (See Visualization.)

IMPRESSION: An image or symbol mentally received and interpreted intuitively.

INCARNATION: Being born into the physical body to experience life on the earth plane.

INCENSE: A scent used in Ritualistic practices to induce "a good vibrational atmosphere for metaphysical work." Various scents are used for different purposes.

INSPIRATIONAL WRITING: The written channeling of one's <SPIRIT GUIDES & TEACHERS> to obtain information on various matters. In this case, though similar to <AUTOMATIC WRITING>, the hand is not controlled by one's guides.

INTUITION: A hunch or feeling. A sense of knowing without a specific reason.

JOURNAL: A book in which to record various notes and experiences for future reference to determine one's level of psychic development and progress.

KARMA: The law of cause and effect. It refers to a spiritual debt or obligation as a growth lesson needed in order to consider that debt or obligation cancelled or "learned" through the natural evolution of the soul, through each successive physical incarnation.

KIRLIAN PHOTOGRAPHY: A special form of photography which records the auric field of a person, animal, mineral, etc. It registers as colored flares of energy. The energy field is not fixed and changes according to the state of consciousness of the subject at the time the photo is taken.

LAVENDER BUDS: An herb used in <RITUAL> as in ingredient to induce "love or romance." May be brewed in liquid mixtures or used ground up in preparations.

LEAD CRYSTAL: A man-made crystal, composed of lead and sand. It is very dense in physical structure, as well as spiritual vibration. However, it does function as a prism and refracts light and breaks it up into the spectrum.

LIGHT: Clarity of purpose and will. Also used to denote mental wisdom and spiritual insight.

LIFE-FORCE: Pure energy, <PRANA>, the energies of the <UNIVERSE> needed to sustain life in the animal, vegetable, or mineral kingdoms.

LUCID DREAM: A <DREAM> in which the subject consciously realizes that he is dreaming, without disturbing the natural sequence of the dream.

MAGNETIC THERAPY: The process or technique of restoring the body's natural magnetic <ALIGNMENT>. It is most commonly performed on people. However, it may also be used in conjunction with the animal, vegetable, or mineral kingdoms.

MAGNETIZED: That which is prepared or energized for the attraction of certain energies.

MAGNETIZED CLOTH: A cloth that has been magnetically charged with energy for the purpose of sending healing energy.

MAGNETISM: Attracting capabilities for various types of energies.

MASTER TEACHERS: Those who, while on the earth plane, reached the highest levels of <SPIRITUAL> and <METAPHYSICAL> attainment of knowledge; who in spirit form, are able to return to the earth plane from other dimensions, in order to teach those in need and who desire to learn and progress spiritually.

MEDITATION: The act of freeing or <CLEARING> the mind from all distractions to the point of the exclusion of all thought.

MENTAL PROJECTION: To mentally place one's consciousness in a given object or at a given location. It is a way of mentally sending thoughts or energies to a desired locale.

METAPHYSICAL HEALING: The art of healing through the power of the mind in combination with the <ALIGNMENT> of the body's electrical energies through <MAGNETIC THERAPY>.

METAPHYSICS: A way of life which utilizes the ability of the mind to create or manifest what is needed through the power of positive thinking and the use of the <PSYCHIC> senses. Also refers to that which is above or beyond the physical realm.

MINT: An herb used as an ingredient in <RITUAL> to refresh the energy. It is also stimulating but soothing to the mind and body. May be brewed in a liquid mixture or ground up and used dry.

MYSTICISM: The practice of using one's inner knowledge or <PSYCHIC> vision to predict events.

NEGATIVE: That which is not constructive or otherwise beneficial and has a detrimental influence or effect upon someone or something.

NEGATIVE HAND: The hand of negative polarity used for <DRAWING OUT> energy during <MAGNETIC THERAPY>.

NEGATIVE POLARITY: One of the poles of an electrical <ENERGY> <CURRENT> of which the primary element is the electron.

NEUTRAL: That which does not affect someone or something in either a <POSITIVE> or <NEGATIVE> way.

NEUTRAL POLARITY: The exact center, or balance point between the <POSITIVE> and <NEGATIVE> poles, of which the primary element is the neutron.

NUMEROLOGY: A type of <READING> based on the study of numbers in direct relation to one's birth date and the numerical value of the letters in a name and how they affect one's life.

OBSESSION: Excessive mental, emotional, and physical preoccupation with something, or someone.

OCCULT: That which is mysterious or concealed. Deals with the "Secret Knowledge" that pertains to the supernatural.

OLIVE OIL: Used in <RITUAL> as an all-purpose <ANOINTING OIL> for <CANDLE DRESSING>.

OUIJA BOARD: A board with the alphabet, numbers, and symbols on it. It is placed between two people, who place their fingers lightly on a planchette, which moves around the board spelling out messages. It is generally believed that the messages are from the spirit plane.

PALMISTRY: A type of <READING> based on the study of the lines in the hand. It is used to determine personality characteristics and the possibility of various outcomes in one's life.

PARAPSYCHOLOGY: Scientific investigation dealing with various aspects of psychic phenomena such as telepathy, psychokinesis, <CLAIRVOY-ANCE>, and <PRECOGNITION>.

PARSLEY: An herb used as in ingredient in <RITUAL> to induce a "calming affect or to influence matters for the better." May be brewed in a liquid mixture or used dry.

PAST LIVES: Previous life times, or <INCARNATIONS> experienced on the earth plane. Also a form of psychic reading, whereby the reader focuses his attention on the querent, allowing thoughts and impressions to come to mind. The imagery is then related to the querent.

PAST LIFE REGRESSION: The act of being regressed or mentally taken back in time through one's current life or previous <INCARNATIONS>. This is usually done through some form of <HYPNOSIS> or creative <VISUALIZATION>.

PENDULUM: This method of <READING> is used for obtaining answers to "yes" and "no" questions. A small object is attached to a piece of cotton twine. It is then held over the written question and allowed to swing back and forth until an answer is indicated by either a clockwise or counterclockwise motion.

PINE OIL: An <ANOINTING OIL> used in <RITUAL> for protection against <NEGATIVE ENERGIES>.

PLAYING CARDS: The use of a regular deck of playing cards to determine the future. Each card separately and in combination with the others, depicts different aspects of one's life. Can also be used for testing one's intuitive ability, by having the subject try to psychically determine the color and/or the suit of the card being presented. This is done with the subject's eyes closed.

POLARITY: This refers to two poles of energy that are in complete opposition to one another, so as to create an <ELECTROMAGNETIC> effect.

POLARITY BALANCING: Creating the proper balance of <NEGATIVE> and <POSITIVE> energies.

POSITIVE: That which in some manner is beneficial to someone or something.

POSITIVE HAND: The hand of <POSITIVE POLARITY> used for <PUTTING IN ENERGY> during <MAGNETIC THERAPY>. Normally, also the hand which matches the <DOMINANT EYE>.

POSITIVE POLARITY: One of the poles of an electrical <ENERGY CURRENT> of which the primary element is the proton.

PRANA: Pure energy. The <LIFE-FORCE> necessary to sustain life.

PRECOGNITION: <PSYCHIC> perception of an event prior to its occurrence.

PREMONITION: A sense of knowing something, without apparent reason, before it happens.

PROGRAMMING: To place a thought in the subconscious mind.

PSYCHE: From the Greek language, meaning "the soul." Also refers to the mind.

PSYCHIC: The process of relating messages strictly on an intuitive basis by interpreting thoughts that are mentally received and the translation of visions and their <SYMBOLOGY>.

PSYCHIC ATTACK: <NEGATIVE> thoughts, actions and energies sent to someone consciously or subconsciously, which in some manner are able to influence or control that individual.

PSYCHIC CHANNELING: (See Channeling).

PSYCHIC PROTECTION: That which protects from psychic negativity. The <WHITE LIGHT> is commonly used throughout the text as a synonymous term for protection.

PSYCHIC SURGERY: (See Body-Enterings).

PSYCHOMETRY: A type of <READING> performed by receiving and sensing impressions. This is accomplished by holding and/or viewing an object.

PUTTING IN ENERGY: To pass energy into someone or something. This may be done manually, as in <MAGNETIC THERAPY> or mentally through thought projection.

PYRAMID ENERGY: The type of energy field experienced in the "Great Pyramid of Giza" — in Egypt, which is able to generate and send energy to any object placed near its vicinity. However, the greatest energy is generated directly below the apex.

QUARTZ CRYSTAL: A natural mineral, used as a gemstone, having the ability to function as a transmitter, amplifier, and a receiver of energy.

QUERENT: The person who is having the <READING> and asking the questions.

RADIATE: To emit rays or energy.

READING: To predict or foretell the events in one's life.

RECEIVER: Refers to a person or an object capable of receiving various types of energy for future use. (Also see Telepathic Receiving.)

RECEIVING HAND: (See Negative Hand.)

RECURRING DREAM: A dream which repeats or occurs in exactly the same manner each time.

REINCARNATION: To be born again with the same soul into a new physical embodiment.

REM SLEEP STATE: REM are the initials for Rapid Eye Movement. Refers to a sleep state occurring approximately 90 minutes after sleep begins, during which, the person is said to be experiencing the imagery of his dreams. The eye movements can be observed, and because of this fact, a great deal of research has been done on the subject of sleep.

RITUAL: An established format for a ceremony including any words spoken, or actions necessary for completion of the act.

ROSEMARY: An herb used as an ingredient in <RITUAL> to induce "protection against negativity." May be brewed in a liquid mixture or ground up and used dry.

RUNES: This <READING> style utilizes stones containing the various letters from an ancient Scandinavian (Viking) alphabet script. Each letter pertains to a specific philosophy of life. As each Rune is drawn, it becomes a direct response to one's questions.

SAGE: A spice used as an ingredient in <RITUAL> to promote "wisdom." It may be brewed in a liquid mixture or used dry.

SALT: A spice used as an ingredient in <RITUAL> to "draw out negativity and purify." It may be added to liquid mixtures or used dry.

SAND: This method of <READING> is strictly based on one's intuitive abilities. The reader allows thoughts and impressions to come to him by focusing on the imprinted patterns in the sand that have been made by the <QUERENT>.

SENDER: (See Telepathic Sending.)

SENSING: To have sensitivity to, or awareness of, something on a conscious or <PSYCHIC> level.

SILVER CORD: The <PSYCHIC> connecting link between man's physical body and his <ETHERIC DOUBLE>, which enables him to return to the physical body from a state of <ASTRAL PROJECTION>.

SPIRIT GUIDES: Spirit forms or energies that work from other dimensions to help us in our personal lives as well as to assist us in attaining a higher level of spiritual growth.

SPIRIT TEACHERS: (See Spirit Guides.)

SPIRITUAL: (Spirit/Ritual) A ritualistic approach to the personal development of the soul, calling upon the assistance of one's personal <SPIRIT GUIDES & TEACHERS>, as well as other <DIVINE> energies of the <UNIVERSE>. (Not necessarily in the religious or <SPIRITUALIST> context.)

SPIRITUAL ALTAR: An area, or surface, upon which to place articles such as candles, <INCENSE>, <ANOINTING OILS>, <FLOWERS>, pictures, crystals, and other gems, as well as any other symbolic items which enhance one's energy for spiritual devotion.

SPIRITUAL BATH: A ritualistic bath prepared for the purpose of reinforcing the spiritual energies around oneself in order to accomplish or bring about a desired effect.

SPIRITUALISM: (See Trance Mediumship.)

SPIRITUALIST: (See Trance Mediumship.)

SYMBOLOGY: Images or symbols representing certain objects or ideas.

TALISMAN: An object that is worn or carried on the person as a symbol of "good luck."

TAROT CARDS: This method of <READING> uses 78 pictured cards.Each card depicts a portion of the events in one's life. In combination with each other, they tell the story as a whole.

TEA LEAVES: This method of <READING> requires that the <QUERENT> drink a cup of tea. There are a series of patterns and corresponding meanings used to interpret the leaves that are left in the bottom of the cup. Loose tea must be used.

TELEPATHIC RECEIVING: The perception that one is receiving a thought transmission, whether consciously, or at the subconscious level.

TELEPATHIC SENDING: The sending of a thought transmission to a designated person or place.

THIRD EYE: May be thought of as a <PSYCHIC> eye or visionary center. Though not visible with the physical eyes, it is located between them, about an inch above the level of the eyebrows. This is the 6th <CHAKRA>, and is used to "see" the mental imagery of the dream state. The development of this center is called "Opening the Third Eye."

THOUGHT FORMS: The etheric form and energy created by the transmission of a thought.

TRANCE: (See Trance Mediumship.)

TRANCE MEDIUMSHIP: The ability to <CHANNEL> one's <SPIRIT GUIDES & TEACHERS> by bringing them into the physical body of the medium, while in an <ALTERED STATE> called a trance. In this manner they may verbally communicate with others to share knowledge of the <ASTRAL PLANES> and to answer questions.

TRANSMITTER: A device, or object, capable of sending or transferring energies from one person or place to another.

TRANSMUTATION: The alteration or change of the structural properties of matter or energy.

UNIVERSE: Referring to the world, as well as other dimensional planes or <ETHERS>. Also refers to the forces of creation, "God."

VIBRATION: A wave of energy which takes on mental, physical, and emotional densities by the intensity and frequency of its oscillation, within a specific time frame.

VIBRATORY RATE: The speed at which energy moves through time and dimension.

VIOLET FLAME: A purifier of <PSYCHIC> <NEGATIVITY>. Also having the quality of <TRANSMUTATION> due to its color and <VIBRATION>.

VISUALIZATION: The act of mentally seeing pictures and images without the aid of physical sight, but rather through the use of the <THIRD EYE>.

WALNUTS: Used in <RITUAL> as an ingredient in various preparations to induce "the end or rather the severing of a tie or relationship." May be boiled in the shell whole, or used ground up dry.

WATER: Used in <RITUAL> as a main ingredient in most liquid preparations to induce "clarity of mind and purpose, as well as being a cleansing agent." All types of water may be used in ritual with the exception of <DISTILLED WATER> and bottled water. These are deionized and not suited for spiritual work.

WHITE LIGHT: White symbolizes purity, cleansing and protection. The concept of <LIGHT> is used for the purpose of creating a visual image to use while protecting oneself psychically.

WHITE MAGIC: Referring to the concept of performing some type of <RITUAL>. Always performed for the highest and best interests of all persons concerned.

YARROW LEAVES: An herb used in <RITUAL> as an ingredient in various preparations to induce "love and romance." May be brewed in liquid mixtures or added dry.